"What a delight to read *Work*, reflecting the depth of talent and commitment of Latine social workers serving communities, bringing healing, mobilizing for change, and celebrating the cultural pride that binds and grounds us, for our own progress and the progress of Hispanic people everywhere. This volume highlights a cyclical pattern of planting and harvesting, and planting again, experienced in the narratives of social work professionals that give back, as they learn and grow professionally, sowing into up-and-coming social workers, who themselves will sow into the next generation. This third volume is a mentorship edition, focused on how we grow and build capacity within the profession, lifting up the people, the issues, and the progress we strive for. This third volume speaks to our progress, and the role of mentoring in advancing it. It represents the power of valuing communities, professional communities, familial communities, neighborhood communities, and more. We are on our knees, not begging, but rather sowing into rich soil, lovingly cultivating what will be a bountiful harvest that will nourish us and help us grow. This is what it means to heal and empower ourselves, and yet not stop at ourselves. This is why we exclaim *"Pa'lante!"*

Onward! For us, for the next generation, and for those yet to come."

Dr. Linda Lausell Bryant, MSW, Ph.D

Associate Dean of Academic Affairs and Clinical Professor at NYU Silver School of Social Work

---

"As I read these authors' deeply personal narratives, I am struck by how their stories reflect so many of the challenges faced by Latinx communities, but also how they highlight the profound strength and resilience that can emerge from such experiences. These journeys feel like a powerful mirror to many of the struggles and triumphs that the Latine community has had to endure. It's not just a story about overcoming obstacles—it's a story about finding purpose through those obstacles, about using the pain as fuel for advocacy, healing, and justice.

These narratives highlight a truth I've come to understand in my own work: there is a unique power in leadership that is grounded in lived experience. Authors' journeys prove that the best social workers—and the best leaders—are those who understand the systems of oppression they seek to challenge, not only through theory or training but through their very own lives. They reaffirm why it's so critical to have more Latine voices in executive roles—voices that can bring their cultural knowledge, their lived experience, and their commitment to justice into spaces where decisions are made.

Like the authors, I believe leadership rooted in compassion, cultural humility, and a commitment to justice can drive real, lasting change. This is the kind of leadership I strive to embody and encourage in others, especially in fields where systemic bias and cultural misunderstandings are rampant.

I am grateful for these stories, as they serve as a poignant reminder of why we need more Latinx leaders, especially in executive positions within fields like social work. It is important to remember that leadership is not just about credentials or titles, but about having the courage to stand up for those who are often not a priority and advocating for policies that center on equity, cultural relevance, and long-term change."

With Gratitude and Hope!

Claudia Boyle, LMHC

Chief Executive Officer, Hispanic Counseling Center

"As a first-generation Ecuadorian social worker, I know firsthand the challenges and triumphs that come with navigating this field. For many of us, mentorship is not just a support system; it is a lifeline. *Latinx/e in Social Work, Vol. III: Mentorship Edition* truly captures the essence of what it means to have someone guide you through the complexities of social work, especially when there are so few role models who look like us in this profession.

Reading these powerful narratives, I am reminded of the incredible strength and resilience that exists within our community. The stories of mentees, Madrinas/Padrinos, and Emerging Leaders highlight not only the personal growth that comes from mentorship, but also the collective power we hold when we come together. These stories are inspiring, and they offer hope and healing, particularly for those of us who have often felt isolated or unheard in a profession that has historically overlooked us.

This book is a call to action. It's time to make a change. We cannot afford to gatekeep the wisdom, experiences, and support that our community needs. As Latinx/e social workers, we must continue to build bridges, not walls. We need to support each other, lift each other up, and ensure that future generations have the tools, mentorship, and resources to thrive. This volume is more than just a collection of stories—it is a movement.

I am proud to be part of this movement, and I urge everyone in the social work field to read these stories, share them, and, most importantly, take action. Together, we can transform the profession and create spaces where Latinx/e social workers not only survive, but flourish."

Paula Medina, LMSW

"This book is a powerful testament to the resilience, passion, and dedication of Latinx social workers. It captures their cultural values and the vital role they play in fostering change. It's a must-read for understanding the intersection of identity, advocacy, and community care through the stories of Latinx social workers."

D'Andrah Almanzar, LMSW

"As I reflect on the stories I've read from this volume of *Latinx/e in Social Work,* I am moved and inspired by the raw authenticity pouring out of each narrative. Latinx/e in Social Work offers a space for social workers who look and sound like me to experience a sense of liberation regarding the injustices and hardships many of my colleagues have faced, overcome, and harnessed to inform their approach to the work. When it comes to personal and collective healing, it is not simply the act of recognizing that we have made it through the fire, but also allowing ourselves the grace to share those moments of trial and tribulation with the purpose of collectively owning our narrative and sharing that wisdom with those who continue to show up every day and do the work. At the end of the day, I recognize that I am a tool within the work, which means that in order for me to show up as authentically as I can—allowing the work to happen—I have a responsibility to myself, my village, and those I serve to nurture and honor my authenticity through spaces such as *Latinx/e in Social Work.* These narratives remind me that I am not "overreacting," and that my struggles are my truth, and they are valid."

Karla Vanessa Herrera, LCSW

"As a Dominican immigrant and social worker, I see our work as a collective effort to liberate and decolonize mental health care. This book amplifies the voices and experiences of Latinx/e social workers who strive to blend culturally resonant practices with traditional therapy. Together, they acknowledge our community's struggles while honoring our resilience and wisdom, moving toward more inclusive and transformative healing."

Farah Reynoso, MSW, RYT

Latinx/e in SOCIAL WORK®

Stories that heal, inspire and connect communities

VOL. III - *Mentorship Edition*

ERICA PRISCILLA SANDOVAL, LCSW, SIFI

LATINX/E IN SOCIAL WORK VOL. III

For more information, contact:
Latinx in Social Work | www.latinxinsocialwork.com
Fig Factor Media, LLC | www.figfactormedia.com

Cover Design & Layout by LDG Juan Manuel Serna Rosales

Printed in the United States of America

ISBN: 978-1-961600-01-0
Library of Congress Control Number: 2022916850

Dedicated to all mentors and mentees who inspire, guide, and support each other on the journey of personal growth and development. Your commitment to learning and teaching creates a powerful bond that uplifts and empowers us all. Thank you for your dedication and guidance.

TABLE OF CONTENTS

Our Trees: Intergenerational Trauma and Post-Traumatic Growth

Our Leaves: Complexity, Legacy, and the Beauty of Transformation

ACKNOWLEDGMENTS

Latinx/e in Social Work has been and continues to be a labor of love. First and foremost, I want to thank God and all my spiritual guides for giving me the strength to grow and heal. You have provided me with the support and resilience to navigate my journey.

Thank you to the *Latinx/e in Social Work* team: Laura A. Alonzo, Mia Edelstein, and Sarah Terrazano. This book would not exist without their tireless efforts behind the scenes. Thank you to our Social Media Coordinator, Brigette Bertoni. Thank you to the team at Fig Factor Media for understanding our vision of this incredible book and helping us make it a reality.

My deepest gratitude to Dr. Anthony T. Estreet for writing the Foreword, to Dianne Morales for the Introduction, and to Lynda Perdomo-Ayala for the Afterword.

Thank you to the conferences and organizations that allow us to share this book and present our work: the National Association of Social Workers (NASW), the National Latinx Psychological Association (NLPA), the Council on Social Work Education (CSWE), and the New York State Social Work Education Association (NYSSWEA).

To the brave, amazing authors who trusted my vision and embarked on this journey together: thank you. Three volumes in, I am still in awe at your resilience, courage, and growth, and the love and honor for our identities and experiences you pour into your narratives. You are all extraordinary, you are all revolutionary, and without all of you, there would be no *Latinx/e in Social Work.* Thank you for being vulnerable, courageous thought leaders. We are making a difference. To the founding authors of Volume I and the inspiring authors of Volume II, thank you for paving the way for Volume III.

Starting the nonprofit Siembra Today with fellow *Latinx/e in Social Work* authors is one of my proudest accomplishments and is a culmination of our resilience, hope, and healing. Thank you to our incredible Board of Directors and staff.

I want to thank our readers—the social justice change agents, the students, the social workers, the educators, and the trailblazers—for reading our narratives and sharing your kind words with us. We know this is not easy, and we hope our narratives help you feel less isolated and more supported. You are the reason we continue this work. You are not alone. Pa'lante!

This volume is dedicated to all the mentors I've had throughout my life—personal, professional, and ancestral. Thank you to Dr. Linda Lausell Bryant, my madrina in social work, and to my mother, grandmother, and great-grandmother who came before me.

Above all, thank you to my family, Nick and Isabella. Every night when I come home, I am grateful for the love I have that recharges me to get back up and keep going.

Erica Priscilla Sandoval, LCSW, SIFI

Foreword

Dr. Anthony T. Estreet, Ph.D., MBA, LCSW-C

In our ever-changing world filled with growing social challenges and opportunities, the role of social workers has never been more essential. Social work is more than a job—it is a commitment to fighting for equity and justice through direct practice, thoughtful policy, and strong advocacy. For the Latinx/e community, this field is also responsible for representing and telling the stories that shape our shared experiences. This is where Latinx/e in Social Work finds its purpose, standing as a testament to the strength of storytelling and a powerful tool for inspiring leadership that lifts individuals and their communities.

As part of this field, I have seen firsthand the impact of storytelling. Our stories are more than personal journeys; they are threads woven into a larger fabric of resilience, pride, and hope. This book celebrates that fabric, inviting readers to recognize the strength of the Latinx community in social work—both in practice and spirit.

THE POWER OF STORYTELLING

Storytelling has always been one of the most genuine ways to share knowledge and experiences. For generations, it has been at the core of Latinx culture, a way to pass down history, values, and identity. In social work and leadership, storytelling is not just meaningful, it is transformative. The stories in this book highlight the struggles and successes of the authors and call for the change those experiences demand.

Each narrative offers a glimpse into the real-life experiences of Latinx social workers—the challenges, victories, and moments that changed their trajectories. These stories build bridges between professional practice and reality, fostering empathy and understanding while serving as catalysts for social change. They remind us that behind every policy and practice lies a human story that needs to be heard.

For Latinx social workers and those aspiring to join the field, these stories offer validation and strength, celebrating shared heritage and encouraging self-belief. For those outside the community, they open the door to empathy and a deeper understanding of the unique challenges Latinx professionals face, both in social work and the communities they serve.

THE IMPORTANCE OF MENTORSHIP AND SPONSORSHIP

Becoming an effective, compassionate social worker is often marked by uncertainty and obstacles. For Latinx individuals, the journey can be even more challenging—navigating underrepresented spaces, facing systemic biases, and balancing personal and professional identities. In this landscape, mentorship is not just helpful but crucial.

Mentorship offers guidance, support, and belonging. It allows new Latinx social workers to learn from those who have navigated similar paths, sharing lessons and strategies for resilience. Sponsorship, on the other hand, takes it a step further. It uses one's influence to create opportunities—advocating for someone when decisions are made, pushing for recognition, and opening doors that may otherwise remain closed.

These stories remind us that behind many successful social workers are people who believed in their potential and advocated on their behalf. While mentorship empowers individuals to find their voices, develop their leadership skills, and inspire others to do the same, sponsorship helps address the systemic challenges many Latinx professionals face. It ensures that those who rise to leadership positions reflect the diverse communities they serve.

BUILDING A LEGACY

Latinx/e in Social Work is more than a collection of personal narratives; it's a call to action. It encourages the Latinx community and its allies to step into roles as mentors, sponsors, and storytellers. This book aims to cultivate a lasting legacy where future generations of Latinx social workers thrive in environments that value their voices and contributions.

Social work is fundamentally about people—meeting them where they are and journeying alongside them. For Latinx social workers, this mission is further enriched by cultural identity, resilience, and a commitment to lifting those who follow. This book stands as a testament to these values, reminding us of the importance of sharing our stories, mentoring the next generation, and advocating for those ready to lead.

I invite you to read these stories not just as individual

experiences but as a collective call to action. May they serve as beacons of hope and inspiration, highlighting the power within our community. Let them encourage you to share your own story, adding to the legacy we continue to build.

Anthony T. Estreet, Ph.D., MBA, LCSW-C
Chief Executive Officer
National Association of Social Workers

INTRODUCTION
Dianne Morales

The publication of this book on the heels of the 2024 US Presidential election is both timely and hopeful. The stories captured in this volume speak to times of adversity as well as the power of the human spirit and our communities in the face of seemingly insurmountable odds. Their journeys tell the age-old tale of generations that have overcome barriers and the depths of despair when circumstances might otherwise seem hopeless. Yet our community always finds a path forward, ensuring a way to "lift as (we) climb."

Even as we live through challenging times that threaten human and civil rights locally and globally, these stories offer a glimmer of hope that pierces the darkness, bringing forth the best in ourselves and, in doing so, encouraging the best parts of our history to repeat itself. The experiences shared by these authors demonstrate that our paths are inextricably linked. The good of the collective benefits us all because the whole is truly greater than the sum of its parts.

I wrote the following on the morning of November 6, 2024, for our authors, for the generations before them, and for those to come who will continue to build upon the strength of our community. To acts of joy and resistance, big and small:

"It stormed here last night in Dorado, Puerto Rico. The loud, angry rumbling shook me from my fitful sleep, demanding my attention and shaking off any notion of escape from the dawn of harsh reality. Consciousness burst in, reminding me of the darkness I'd sought to ignore. I felt the collective grief of the earth assemble and rise as the rumblings grew slowly, roiling and building into explosions that vibrated through the atmosphere, demanding to be heard, signaling the transgressions of the moment and the self-defeating choices made by men.

Sharp cracks of light followed, burning through the night. Lashes that cut into the depths of our open wound of mourning, at once reflecting and affirming our pain even as they admonish having been forsaken. The sky grieving and angry, opened up to unleash while threatening to swallow us whole. Unnerved by the disturbance, I was shaken to my core. Then I wrapped myself in its darkness and sunk into the comfort of its depths, enveloped in rage and despair, and let go.

This morning, I rose unsettled, numb with an overwhelming sense of despair, struggling to cling onto hope or even a ray of possibility that may not come today.

Today I will mourn. I will scream into the void. I will surround myself with loved ones and small acts of kindness. I will retreat.

Tomorrow will come regardless. And it will be filled with new-old battles. I will not retreat. I will not shrink. I will not fold to the will of the darkness that seeks to stomp out the light.

Instead, I will drink from the well of strength of the ancestors that surround me. Those who propelled me to this moment, and on whose shoulders I stand. And I will return to the struggle once again, to fight for the rights of those who would strip me of my own. I will return with love and strength and power. And I will carry on with the hopes of justice for us all. One day."

Pa'lante, in solidarity,

Dianne Morales
Founder and President
StillRising

MADRINA & PADRINO

We name and identify social work leaders as a *"madrina"* or *"padrino"* (godmother or godfather). A madrina or padrino acts as a mentor, sponsor, patroness, or supporter to our growth, career, and profession. They lead the way, open and create space, pass the baton, and help us grow and thrive. Volume III features the narratives of 13 madrinas/padrinos (mentors) and their 13 mentees.

In this volume, we also amplify the voices of three Emerging Leaders, social workers just starting out in their careers with bright futures ahead in the field. We also include the narrative of our founder, Erica Priscilla Sandoval, LCSW.

Together, these 30 narratives honor the crucial role that mentorship plays for social workers, mental health practitioners, and professionals. The spaces we create and nurture in mentorship, and the blossoming relationships that follow, are vital to the growth and development of future Latinx/e leaders.

WHAT ARE MENTORSHIP AND SPONSORSHIP?

Volume III: Mentorship Edition highlights the transformative impact of mentorship in the social work field. For Latinx/e social workers, especially from first-generation families, a mentor provides guidance and hope in a profession lacking Latinx/e role models to look up to.

Mentorship is guidance, support, sharing resources, giving advice, and sharing personal stories of resilience and success. Mentors can have various roles both professionally and personally. A mentor could be your professor, boss, colleague, friend, community elder, and more.

Sponsorship is often the next step to mentorship. If mentors pave the way, sponsors open doors. Sponsors help with career advancement and advocate for your skills. They say your name in rooms you're not in, recommend you for open positions, and take an active role in your growth.

Both mentorship and sponsorship offer crucial support for new social workers, especially in the Latinx/e community. May this book help show readers that mentors can be found even when you least expect it.

Author Chapters

LEADERSHIP Y LA MAREA: FEELING DIZZY AND FINDING BALANCE

ERICA PRISCILLA SANDOVAL, LCSW, SIFI

"Nothing can dim the light that shines from within."
—Maya Angelou

TU LUZ

The Amazon jungle is a place of self-discovery. I learned this firsthand while in Peru for an Ayahuasca ceremony, where I was supposed to be sitting in silence with my own thoughts. It was one of the most challenging moments in my life. Neurodivergent minds can be very entertaining, and my thoughts kept me company. I could not turn them off—I read 3 books, filled up a journal, and during some down time, just laid in the hammock and wept.

I cried for the little girl I was healing, I cried for my daughter, I cried for my womb that held so much pain for others, and I cried because I allowed myself to. I counted my Ayahuasca ceremonies and tried not to compare the six journeys to each other. I felt light, at ease, serene, and hopeful. I realized how hypersensitive I have been to criticism, especially my own. After achieving some clarity, I was now left to integrate what came up for me into my life.

When I reached Iquitos and returned to the luxurious hotel after spending 10 nights in a hut, I took a long hot shower and was looking forward to having lunch with the beautiful group that had sat with plant medicine together. When I finally had Wi-Fi, I turned on my phone to check some messages. To my surprise, alerts from a colleague popped up, sharing that I was going to be in the New York Post. Me, in the New York Post—why?

Little did I know this was going to be the hardest return to real life a person can have after an Ayahuasca ceremony. The shock was something I never felt before, especially because it was not a kind article. I was being attacked for hosting a seminar for the NYC teacher's union on the harmful effects of whiteness, meant to teach participants about white privilege, internalized racism, microaggressions, and cultural humility. Never did I think that this workshop would receive such criticism, especially from a large news outlet. This is not to mention that nowhere in the article did they say that I was a social worker, an author, a healer, or a business owner. I was described as a "self-proclaimed" DEI leader, language that is inherently meant to undermine.

The article was a punch to the gut, and I felt I had nowhere to turn. I wanted to go back to my hut in the Amazon, where I felt safe from the world. *Is this what it feels like to be a leader?* I wondered. I looked for solace from others in my life, and to my surprise, few stood by my side. This is unfortunately all too common—people distance themselves when things are not going well, but when things are great, they stand beside you. Luckily, I called on my mentors, each of whom gave me incredible advice: keep doing what you are doing; this means you are making a difference. Do not hide, you have nothing to fear. You are a change agent in a political climate where DEI is not welcome. One of the best encouragements was, "Erica, you are making a difference and now you are a public figure. Hold your head up high."

SIEMBRA

As you begin to enter spaces that are not welcoming to people of color, you will have to shield yourself with education, facts, receipts, community, and ancestral wisdom. For me, I find solace in my community of healers. My holistic practices have protected, cleansed, and invigorated me time and time again. I remember being told by my holistic teachers about the many distractions meant to deter me from my path, but that the goal is to stay on track despite these obstacles. I picture a seed—when nurtured with the right environment, it bursts through soil, grows through the cracks, climbs up the walls. It is unstoppable.

Leadership can look very different. I have met some incredible student leaders in the Latinx Social Work Student Organization (LSWSO) at New York University, Silver School Of Social Work. They connect with partners and develop programs and relationships to meet the needs of the student body. I love witnessing their passion and excitement for what they do. If we could bottle up that passion and sprinkle it around people who have been in the field longer, who have become stressed, resentful, and complacent with the bare minimum, we would harvest an endless supply of opportunity.

Through *Latinx/e In Social Work*, I built my own community. Back in 2020, when the world shut down and we were overcome by loneliness, this collective saved many of us. Since the first volume, I have been privileged to bear witness to the amazing growth of each founding author from this series. They have become new mothers, entered into academia, began their clinics, launched their businesses, started nonprofits, been promoted, and even become mentors to others.

And this past year, incredible authors from the *Latinx/e in Social Work* collective and I came together to found the nonprofit Siembra Today. We planted a seed by sharing our personal narratives of trauma, resilience, and healing, and that seed has grown into a women- and BIPOC-led nonprofit dedicated to providing and destigmatizing mental health and wellness support in our communities.

Throughout your career, you may become resentful, jealous, or competitive instead of graceful, selfless, and collaborative.

I invite you to stay the course. As the air thins at the top, you will need someone to pass you your oxygen mask. We must uplift each other and honor each other's unique light. When we blend our gifts, we become extremely powerful as a collective, with the potential to heal the ancestral wounds we may carry along our journey.

I urge you to find your people, nurture your surroundings, be vulnerable, and ask for support when things get rough. You will know who your people are—they will find you too.

CHARCUTERIE BOARD

Community is key when riding the wave. You are going to need a life preserver, someone who can sail, a captain who teaches others to be captains, and a person who can navigate. Imagine how a cruise line runs, with everyone working together. Community is more than the sum of its parts; it is everyone's unique strengths aligning to create something greater.

I began my career as a medical social worker at a specialized hospital. The social work team was the closest connection to family you could have outside of a home. My sister even worked with me, and it felt amazing to have best friends at work. There was some friction, but because of our community, I could move past it with grace. This job taught me an important lesson: build your community, and everything will feel less stressful.

The nonprofit job I had after was not as great when it came to workplace culture. I advanced straight to Director in a white space where I was the only Latina as well as the only social worker. It took many years to build my team, become respected for my professional experience, and foster community. When it was time to move on, I gave a sufficient month's notice and worked tirelessly to create a transition plan, remembering how unsafe and overwhelmed I had felt by my COO's termination. Yet this plan was ignored and their anger at my departure was toxic. Lesson learned? Owning your power and mastering your gifts is key to growth. You are the force that drives change; no one can replicate your work, your education will never be taken away, and those credentials matter.

Now with a salary twenty thousand dollars higher, I was in a Senior Director position at another nonprofit organization, and my head was spinning. I was not aware that our CEO had been diagnosed with breast cancer and she was putting things in place as her health was compromised. During my time with her, I learned how important it is to build a team that loves you, protects you, and cares about your mission and vision. Our CEO was special; she was the face of the organization and her team loved her. Yet they loved her so much, they would do anything to be her go-to person. This created a hostile work environment and psychological safety was compromised. I learned to lean into discomfort and navigate your own ship, even when facing a storm. I helped her transition me out in the midst of the pandemic as we had to make budget cuts. I prepared for my next adventure—I took a two week vacation, finally took the LCSW exam, and passed. Private practice was calling me.

So, how did I get into private practice and accumulate the

clinical hours while working in all these different positions? Where did I get my experience? For 7 years, I worked part-time at Western Queens Consultation in Queens on nights and weekends. I was so proud to work as a therapist for my Queens community. It brought me incredible satisfaction to give back, and every person there taught me so much and left an imprint in my heart.

Fast forward, and now I support a team of 12 social workers and three holistic practitioners in my group practice, Sandoval CoLab. I also began consulting to fill in gaps for organizations that don't have social workers to support their deliverables. We partner with organizations that hire us for supervision, staff workshops, and retreats, all working together.

All this after being told I "did not have business acumen" by a white, cis, male CEO of a nonprofit I worked at. How do you like me now? I've poured all of myself into systems, organizations, jobs, roles, and initiatives that were not mine. I gave them ideas, created initiatives, and built relationships all to help me realize that a job or title didn't make me who I was—my gifts are what set me apart. And they come with me everywhere I go.

Throughout my various careers, mentorship has been at the forefront of my success. I honor each and every mentor, as I would not be where I am today without their advice, reassurance, guidance, ideas, sponsorship, and friendship. Thank you to my supervisor Mavis Seehaus, who helped in signing my clinical hours; to Dr. Edith Chaparro for helping me pass my licensing exam; and to John Lavin, Paul Deasy, and Linda Joannidis from Western Queens Consultation. Because of their support, I obtained my LCSW and embarked on a beautiful journey of serving our community with mental health and holistic practices. It is a reciprocal relationship; I acknowledge their support and honor them by paving the way for others.

What is my niche? It is serving the community I love. It is bringing holistic practices to the forefront and decolonizing mental health and social work. It is working with psychedelics, a groundbreaking approach to reducing symptoms of PTSD, depression, and anxiety. It is storytelling that supports the healing journey of both the storyteller and the individual reading it. It is public speaking and presenting about the work we do as a collective. It is incorporating yoga, sound healing, and cacao ceremonies as group work. It is working with other Latinas and helping them lean into their power, and creating different strategies to undo the stigma of seeking support.

In our Latine* community, there are many unspoken norms that are handed down from previous generations. It often feels like we have to persevere alone and hoard success, since "there was never enough." We have learned behaviors about not sharing resources or not collaborating, in fear that someone might "take from us." To undo this limiting belief, let's understand that we all have different gifts and skills. At the end of the day, there is no competition. As my Madrina Dr. Linda Lausell Bryant says, "There does not need to be one 'big cheese'—we can all be a charcuterie board."

YOUR COMPASS

Have you ever felt exhausted after an event, workday, or class? There was nothing extraordinary about your day, except you connected with different people. Yet sometimes that isn't as harmless as it seems. In fact, your energy can be easily sapped by what are called energy vampires.

There are different ways to suck energy from those around you. Some people always play the victim card, some have constant critiques, and others manipulate situations in service of a hidden agenda. These relationships are harmful for anyone, but especially for empathic people, who easily become drained by energy vampires.

Perhaps you are an energy vampire yourself without realizing it. Be mindful of your energy and how you show up in spaces. Are you blaming others or have difficulty being accountable? Do you often find yourself over-criticizing others (or yourself)? Do your negative thoughts get in the way of fully living a fulfilling life? Are you constantly surrounded by chaos?

Pay attention to your own spirit. We have to understand our own feelings first, and recognize how unprocessed trauma can manifest as suspicion or mistrust. Do I have clear neutral energy or do I have a charge; what is impacting me from being clear? Work on yourself to reach your highest power. Your intuitive guidance will be your compass in your career and life.

Then, when you walk into a room, you will be more attuned to the different energies around you. It will become easier to scan, feel, and connect with them. Intuition is about listening to the voice of your spirit and trusting its energy reading. With time, we can become skilled at using our innate divine compass. We all have this ability; it is a skill that can be practiced.

In social work, energy exhaustion can take a massive toll on our physical and emotional well-being. It can leave you feeling dizzy, vulnerable, depleted, and even wanting to quit. You may not feel like you have a strong foundation, or that you can't stand up straight.

Find a community that fills your cup and mentors who support you, and move away from energy vampires who dim your brilliance. Recharge, revitalize, and show up authentically with grace. When you put in the work to heal past wounds, you will reach greatness. You are light; step into it and let it shine from your heart.

Ancestral Wisdom:

Cleanse your energy with agua florida. Cleanse your space with palo santo. Mente sana, cuerpo sano.

Journal Prompts:
1. What or who in your life is no longer serving you? How can you make a change?
2. What personal superpowers make you unique and can be used as transferable skills in any position you hold?
3. Do you trust your gut? How can you strengthen your intuition and inner compass?

*People of the Diaspora; People of the Global Majority; BIPOC, Latinx/e

BIOGRAPHY

Erica Priscilla Sandoval, LCSW, SIFI is an award-winning social worker, speaker, executive coach, entrepreneur, podcaster, philanthropist, and author. She is the creator of the book series *Latinx/e in Social Work.*

Erica is most recently the Executive Director of Siembra Today, a women-run, BIPOC-led nonprofit devoted to providing accessible mental health and wellness support through narrative storytelling, books, workshops, healing circles, conferences, and social media campaigns. Siembra Today's goal is to destigmatize and promote mental health and wellness for the Latino/a/x/e and BIPOC community, so that they can plant seeds of hope for themselves and future generations.

Erica is also the founder and CEO of Sandoval Psychotherapy Consultation—known as Sandoval CoLab—which offers talk therapy, ketamine-assisted psychotherapy (KAP), and holistic offerings.

Erica holds a Post Master's in Clinical Adolescent Psychology and a Master's in Social Work from New York University, Silver School of Social Work. As a proud immigrant from Ecuador, her passion is fueled by supporting her community.

Instagram: @ericapriscillas
LinkedIn: https://www.linkedin.com/in/ericapsandoval/
https://www.siembratoday.org/
https://www.ericapriscilla.com/
https://www.sandovalcolab.com/

Our Seeds: Resilience, Migration, and Assimilation

LA MUERTE POR OPRESIÓN: NO PERMISSION OR INVITATION NEEDED

PILAR O. BONILLA, MSW

"Realizing that my experiences, while personal, are also part of a shared history of discrimination, oppression, and future liberation helped me understand the importance of first healing my own traumas and internalized oppression so that I can be more intentional about the changes I wish to bring about."

MY "WHY"

In August 2021, with over 700 deaths reported per day by the CDC, COVID-19 was the third leading cause of death in the United States. Coincidentally, it was around this time that I began my journey as a Master of Social Work student.

Why social work?

In 2020, my *primo hermano* (brother cousin or first cousin) was the first in my family to experience COVID-like symptoms. With sweat pouring down his flushed face from a high fever, my primo hermano took himself to the emergency room, only to return home shortly thereafter because the hospitals in our area were over capacity. A few days later, my *primo hermano* returned to the hospital in a critical state, barely able to breathe, much less stand. He was immediately admitted.

During that time, my parents and I began experiencing COVID-like symptoms as well. While trying to keep my parents and myself alive, I simultaneously maintained constant communication with the doctors, nurses, and hospital staff to better understand my *primo hermano's* condition and relay that information to the rest of my family, enabling us to make informed decisions regarding his care. I researched treatment options and reached out to friends abroad to learn about their respective countries' approaches. Desperate for solutions, I felt that something had to give.

After seven months of fighting for his life, my *primo hermano* was stable enough to be moved to a rehabilitation facility. Unfortunately, our choices were limited to available facilities covered by his health insurance. As a result, my primo hermano was placed in a facility with a less-than-stellar reputation and poor patient reviews from before the pandemic.

A month into his stay, my primo hermano went into septic shock from open wounds on his back due to bedsores. He then fell into a coma and was declared brain-dead. My *primo hermano* died shortly thereafter.

To say that my family and I were devastated would be an understatement. *Mis tías y mi mamá* had lost *un hijo*, and *mis primos* and I had lost *un hermano*. "Devastated" did not capture the depth of our sorrow and pain. I say that my mom and her sisters lost a son and my cousins and I lost a brother because my family is matriarchal. In my culture, collective mothering is common, with cousins often being raised together. The proverb "it takes a village to raise a child" aptly reflects this cultural norm.

My *primo hermano* was not the only casualty of COVID-19 in our family. My tío, my *primo hermano's* father and beloved elder, died a few months prior from COVID-19. I almost died as well, enduring symptoms for four tortuous months before I finally began recovering and developing antibodies. Under normal circumstances, I might have been hospitalized along with my *primo hermano,* but these weren't normal times. What had apparently become normalized, however, were the severe health disparities faced by systematically marginalized communities—disparities that persist in our healthcare system today.

SOCIAL JUSTICE WORKER

So, why social work?

COVID-19 was a reality check, bringing long-ignored issues to light. For me, it was the straw that broke the camel's back. How had we reached this point? How had we gotten to a stage where access to basic human rights—such as housing, food, water, healthcare, and education—became contingent on unjust social, economic, and environmental policies?

For years, as I navigated my own health journey, I questioned whether I was the problem, wondering if I was imagining things or overreacting. So what if it didn't seem right or felt unfair? I was being overly sensitive, wasn't I? This was just happening to me, I told myself. This was perfectly normal, right? Right?!

Wrong.

I had fallen victim to the effects of systematic oppression: doubting my feelings, questioning my instincts, and convincing myself to avoid making waves. The resulting trauma had reduced me to a spectator in my own life—merely existing rather than truly living.

While COVID-19 did not discriminate against whom it attacked, it is undeniable that some of us were more vulnerable to infection and death than others. Social, economic, and environmental factors—such as where we lived, whether we had the ability or privilege to social distance, our health insurance status, and the availability of treatment options—played crucial roles in determining our susceptibility to infection and our chances of survival. While I was tired and frustrated, I was alive, and not everyone was that lucky.

Prior to COVID-19, I had plans of going back to my country of birth, Perú, to train under my friend's uncle, a *curandero* (healer) known for treating illnesses deemed incurable by Western medicine. Sadly, *el curandero* was another victim of the pandemic.

Although my plans to become a *curandera* and bring what I learned back to the United States changed, my commitment to healing remained steadfast. As a member of a discriminated ethnoracial group directly impacted by oppressive systems, I recognized the need for collective healing from the deep and open soul wounds inflicted by the mere existence of myself and others of marginalized identities. This type of healing necessitates structural change grounded in a social justice framework.

Social justice involves addressing and rectifying the oppressive conditions and systems that perpetuate inequity. True collective healing, therefore, requires broad structural change to dismantle these systems of oppression. To me, collective healing is social justice's *razón de ser* (reason to be). I believe that healing is essential to achieving liberation from the various forms of oppression that have become normalized in the United States— oppressions that many of us, myself included, had come to accept as part of American culture.

To affect broad, long-lasting structural change, I needed to develop new skills and tools, which led me to pursue social work, a practice inherently oriented toward social justice work. With this, and several other thoughts in mind, I embarked on my journey as a Master of Social Work student.

"YOU'RE *NOT* LIKE US"

The first time I recall experiencing an -ism was in kindergarten. I had made a new friend and both she and I were waiting for our respective parents to pick us up. When the other little girl's mother arrived first, the little girl excitedly asked her mother if she would arrange a playdate with my mom. Her mother responded, "No." When the little girl asked why, her mother took my arm, held it against her daughter's, and said, "That's why."

It was at this moment that I learned what many Black and Brown children learn at an early age: The melanin in my skin mattered. It made me different; it othered me. When *mi mamá* arrived to pick me up, I was hysterically crying. I remember asking her why we were different and why skin color seemed to matter so much. With tears in her eyes, *mi mamá* explained racism to me.

The second time an -ism greatly impacted me at school was in fifth or sixth grade. I was walking down the hallway when I overheard girls speaking Spanish. I had moved to a new school district and was shocked to meet anyone outside my family who spoke the language. Excitedly, I went up to those three girls and happily shared that I also spoke Spanish and was just like them. The girls looked me up and down, whispering to each other, before one stepped forward and said, "You don't look like us, you don't sound like us, you don't dress like us; you are NOT like us." I was crushed. The experience of ethnocentrism hurt in a different way than racism, but it cut just as deep.

I wish I could say that was the last time I felt othered, but it wasn't. I felt it in middle school when I was stopped by two older "well-meaning" women and was lectured about "my people" having kids young while I was out on a stroll with my nieces. I felt it when *mi mamá* and I went to a new laundromat and people spoke about us in Spanish, assuming we didn't understand because our facial features leaned more towards our Indigenous and Asian ancestors. I felt it whenever someone asked where I was from or used the word "exotic" to describe me. I felt it in college when an older White woman refused to sit at a table with me and my Middle Eastern friend. I felt it when an ex-boyfriend tried to explain how being compared to a coconut—brown on the outside and white on the inside—was actually a compliment.

Even worse were the times I heard people refer to Latinos as roaches, as less than human, as trash that needed to be thrown out and sent back to their countries—conveniently ignoring the United States' role in destabilizing those countries' governments, economies, and environments.

My social work education provided me with the terminology and understanding I needed to explain things I had experienced throughout my life. It was both validating and numbing to know that my experiences were in fact so common that they were parts of textbooks.

I have learned the value of critical thinking and the equally important practice of critical self-reflection. Recognizing the impact of both implicit and explicit biases, in myself and others, was essential to this process. I now understand how my positionality, social identity, and intersectionality as an Indigenous Latine, cisgender, disabled woman profoundly shape my experiences. These factors, combined with my personal history with oppression and discrimination, significantly influence how I engage with and perceive the world, informing my approach to social justice work. Without ongoing critical self-reflection and acknowledgment of the intrinsic links between my experiences, values, and social identity, I risk perpetuating harm, potentially becoming part of the very problem I seek to address. This awareness is key to maintaining the integrity of my commitment to social justice.

Realizing that my experiences, while personal, are also part of a shared history of discrimination, oppression, and future liberation helped me understand the importance of first healing my own traumas and internalized oppression so that I can be more intentional about the changes I wish to bring about. After all, personal healing and collective healing overlap and are interconnected.

IF IT AIN'T BROKE, STILL FIX IT

For a long time, I believed our healthcare system was broken and in desperate need of an overhaul. I've since realized that, like many other systems, it is not broken but rather functioning as it was intended to—failing to serve all individuals equitably. While the creators of these systems may have had the best of intentions, the reality remains that these systems serve the few, not the many. For instance, if our healthcare system were truly effective, from the onset of the pandemic to the present day, the health disparities and high casualty rates from COVID-19 would not be as severe.

Regardless of differing opinions on whether the system is broken, COVID-19 has clearly highlighted that our healthcare system is just one of many interconnected systems that require fixing. We, as individuals, are neither the systems that have been created, nor should we be defined by them. As such, we cannot continue to be passive participants in their operations. As social workers and as a society, we must work together to address this.

Real, broad, and long-lasting structural change cannot be achieved by working in silos, especially in the United States, where Western European settler colonial, white supremacist, capitalist, heteronormative, patriarchal, and neoliberal values and policies dominate. Dismantling systems of oppression requires intentionality and a commitment to collective action—no invitation or permission needed.

CommUNITY

As a newly graduated social worker, I have found community not only with people who share my mother tongue, culture, or identities, but also with those who, through shared experiences of systematic oppression, are united in our commitment to dismantling these systems and creating transformative change. Our shared humanity and the power of unity in the face of life's most daunting obstacles make us that much stronger.

The word "community" contains "unity," signifying the transcendence of unfruitful divisions. Whether intentional or not, this is a powerful reminder that social justice work requires unity among those of us impacted by these systems of oppression. Healing is collective, it's interconnected, and only united can we be liberated.

Without the love, support, and understanding of my family and friends, I doubt I would be here today. Therefore, I cannot overstate the importance of extending grace to yourself and others—never assuming you fully know what someone else is going through. Regardless of the paths we take, we all have the capacity to learn, change, and work in solidarity in the pursuit of justice.

It took years of being told that there was nothing wrong with me—that it was all in my head—and finally being diagnosed with a rare condition for me to question the functionality of our healthcare system. It took standing at the hospital bedside of my *primo hermano*—hearing him take his last breaths while wondering how we ended up there—for me to take action.

Change is difficult, and the progress is often nonlinear, moving forward and backward. Yet, without the hope that together we can heal collectively and create a just and more equitable future, I wouldn't be here today sharing a piece of my story with you.

Thank you, Rosita Marinez, for being an invaluable part of my journey. I am deeply grateful for your guidance and dedication in pushing me to achieve my best. You are an incredible individual with a huge heart and an even greater commitment to doing what is just, not just what is easy. Thank you, Madrina.

Ancestral Wisdom:

Mi mamá always says, "Ser guerreros está en nuestra sangre." (Being warriors is in our blood.)

Journal Prompts:

1. What does it mean to be a social justice worker?

2. How are collective healing and social justice interconnected?

3. How can I decolonize my mind?

BIOGRAPHY

Pilar O. Bonilla, MSW, earned her Master of Social Work degree from Hunter College Silberman School of Social Work. A dedicated social justice advocate, Pilar is actively involved in the Payment for Placements (P4P) movement, the Social Worker Equity Campaign (SWEC), and the #StopASWB Campaign—advocating for racial, gender, and socioeconomic justice through collective action necessary for long-term systemic change.

In her leadership roles, Pilar serves as co-chair of P4P's Advocacy Alliance, a movement that aligns with the broader struggle for dignity and better working conditions for all oppressed workers. Additionally, she is a member of the Social Worker Equity Campaign's steering committee, which is grounded in the principles of equity, unity, and action.

LinkedIn: https://www.linkedin.com/in/pilar-o-bonilla/
IG: https://www.instagram.com/daringly_myself/

SOLEDAD: A NAME OR A CURSE?

CRISTINA CONTRERAS, LMSW, MPA, FABC

"Embrace your solitude, for it is a faithful companion through the darkest of times, guiding you toward a brighter future."

ROOTS OF SOLEDAD

For me, there's an irony in being a social worker. While I love helping people, I frequently feel disconnected from others. "Social" is even in the name of the field of social work, yet I've always experienced a sense of social isolation—a dichotomy between my public life as a civil servant and my private life of unresolved trauma. Reflecting on my upbringing and social work journey, this solitude has been a common thread from childhood to now.

Is it a name or a curse? When I say that solitude has always followed me, I mean it—Soledad is my middle name. Cristina Soledad Contreras. It is fitting for the story I have to tell, for the loneliness and isolation I've felt throughout my life. However, I've come to learn that Soledad does not define me.

I was born in a rough neighborhood to a humble family in the Dominican Republic. Growing up in a dangerous part of Santo Domingo's capital, my grandmother's concern for my safety led to strict rules—I was only permitted to attend school. Childhood memories are sparse; I was forbidden from socializing, attending parties, or even going to church gatherings. Essentially, I felt like a prisoner in my own home. This early isolation set the stage for a lifetime of solitude. Despite having siblings, I felt alone, grappling with shyness and an inability to connect with others.

My mother immigrated to New York with me and my brother when I was 15. However, he and I found ourselves alone shortly after, since my mother had to return to the Dominican Republic as part of her own journey. Living with my 16-year-old brother in rented rooms, and then later alone, I often masked the truth about my living situation, pretending to have stability when the reality was far from it. I knew that if I spoke up, it would only complicate things for my mother even further.

Despite our financial difficulties growing up, my family had always instilled in us that education was a top priority. I quickly learned to see education as a path to freedom, a way out of the environment I was in, and school became like a security blanket.

As a teenager living alone in New York, I continued to see school as a refuge. It was my only constant amidst housing and food insecurity. On some days, school meals were the only way I knew I'd be able to eat. I made sure to arrive early every day for the free breakfast. I clung to the routine, believing that missing a day would unravel everything. Whether that was true or not, I believed it at the time, and didn't want to test the theory.

Despite these challenges, I remained determined. Graduating high school as a teenage mother was a testament to my resilience, proving that amidst adversity, education could be a lifeline. So, while I walked the stage with a diploma, I also carried with me the weight of a child and the scars of a solitary journey.

Childhood and adolescence shaped my solitude, stemming from feelings of abandonment and trust issues. I navigated life feeling like I had no one to rely on, wary of forming connections that might expose my struggles or lead to further pain.

PATH TO SOCIAL WORK

I experienced struggles and difficulties during high school as well as bearing the responsibility of being a mother at an early age. As a minority woman, I also felt that I had to work harder than everyone else to prove I was deserving of success.

My high school had a group therapy pilot program led by a psychologist. It was designed for students with declining grades or other academic setbacks, and I was forced to join. With all the struggles of my home life, my grades had slipped. I was resistant to join the group for obvious reasons; I was terrified that someone would uncover my everyday reality.

But after putting up an initial fight, I wound up flourishing in the program. I became a natural leader in the group, eager to help others and work through their problems—as long as no one was focusing on me. As always, I kept my internal life hidden, even from friends, which only further isolated me. I helped others in the group become more comfortable opening up, and as we talked every week, I watched as this helped them identify the changes they needed to make, both personally and academically.

Encouraged to pursue social work by the psychologist and others in the group, this pilot program was the first seed of my journey in the field. After high school, I went to Lehman College to study social work. I loved it; helping others felt like my calling. I then earned my Master of Social Work from Fordham University, and after graduating I started a job in a hospital. While I've gone through a few career shifts, namely from social work to administration, I've been working in the healthcare industry ever since.

For my entire professional career, it has been easy to throw myself into work. There are a few reasons for this. First, as a minority, I always felt challenged and like I had to prove I deserved a seat at the table. I've faced countless microaggressions based on the intersectionality of my identities as a Black Latina, immigrant, non-native English speaker, and woman. Even in my current position, people question if I deserve to be a CEO because of my background. Second, giving my all to a career reinforced my chronic isolation. I instead focused on helping others, and developed a deep sense of professional isolation in the process. I was constantly working, yet at the same time overlooked for opportunities because of my identity. So I worked harder, and harder, and harder. My soledad only solidified.

It's also true that my experience as a social worker has made me the best administrative leader I can be. No matter what role I'm in, I'm a social worker at heart, which has provided a powerful framework for thoughtful and empathetic leadership. The emotional intelligence I've gained from social work can't be taught in a classroom. It's something I carry with me always, just like my name—even if I've always struggled with the social part of social work.

TURNING POINT

In my journey, I've come to realize that my turning point arrived just a few years ago, long after many others might have experienced theirs. It was a moment of awakening to the generational trauma that had shaped my life for so long. As I reflected on my career and personal struggles, I recognized the profound impact of my past trauma and the isolation it had bred within me.

Consequently, I made a deliberate effort to foster connections with others, something I had previously neglected. I acknowledged the importance of reaching out for support during tough times and began prioritizing my own well-being. This led me to embark on a journey of self-discovery, including starting therapy to unpack the layers of trauma accumulated over the years. Establishing a healthier work-life balance became a priority, and sharing my story within the Latinx social work community was an empowering act of self-care.

Participating in initiatives like Latinx in Social Work and serving as Chair of the National Dominican Day Parade in 2021 has allowed me to reconnect with my heritage and find a sense of belonging that had eluded me in the past. Despite now holding the position of healthcare CEO, being part of a community of social workers remains deeply validating.

Through sharing my experiences, I hope to offer solace to others facing similar struggles, encouraging them to take that crucial first step towards healing and self-improvement. Despite the daunting challenges I've encountered, I've never wavered in my determination to persevere and overcome the solitude that once defined me.

Ancestral Wisdom:

My mom taught me that strength isn't about never being afraid—it's about standing tall in the face of fear, never backing down, and always protecting family and the ones you love.

Journal Prompts:

1. Do the intersectionalities of your identity create differences in your public vs. private personas?
2. Have you felt a connection between isolation, marginalization, and trauma in your own life?

BIOGRAPHY

Born in the Dominican Republic, Cristina Contreras started her career as a caseworker in New York. In 2021, she was appointed as Chief Executive Officer at NYC Health + Hospitals/Metropolitan in East Harlem. Passionate about improving the health of the communities she serves, in this role, Cristina has expanded access to care for underserved populations.

Cristina serves as the Chair of the National Dominican Day Parade, on the Board of the NY Chapter of the Alzheimer's Association, and on the Board of Directors of R.A.I.N. Total Care, Inc.

She holds a Bachelor's in Social Work from Herbert H. Lehman College, a Master's in Social Work from Fordham University, and a second Master's in Public Administration from Baruch College. In 2023, she received the New York College of Podiatric Medicine's honorary degree of Humane Letters, Honoris Causa, at their annual commencement.

EMBRACING REDIRECTION

NATALIE GUTIERREZ, LMSW

"I can be changed by what happens to me. But I refuse to be reduced by it." —Maya Angelou

LITTLE DOMINICAN REPUBLIC

I was born and raised in Washington Heights, also known as "Little Dominican Republic." Washington Heights is a vibrant community rich in Dominican culture, people, and history. Summers consisted of playing in la pompa at Inwood Hill Park and stopping for ices sold from carts. Growing up in a neighborhood that was unapologetically Dominican always made me proud of my roots and ancestry. I came from a neighborhood where my parents knew people from back in their hometowns in Santo Domingo. My grandmother "La Morena" is a beloved 207th Street legend, who is still admired by many in our community for her loving spirit despite moving to Georgia. She was a pillar of our family and community, and always exemplified the importance of being empathetic and sharing resources with others. Looking back now, my grandmother naturally exhibited all the traits of a good social worker.

My parents both hailed from Santo Domingo, Dominican Republic. In the 80s, they both came to New York and settled right by 207th Street in Inwood, a safe space for many Dominican immigrants and the neighborhood that shaped my earliest memories. My parents enrolled at local community colleges for a few semesters. Shortly into their academic careers, they were faced with the brutal realities of struggling to assimilate to a new culture and language. Both my parents withdrew and were unable to complete their college educations.

As a child, pursuing higher education always felt out of my reach. My parents were the strongest people I knew, and I often thought that if they couldn't achieve it, there was no way I could. There was no one to guide me on what that process would look like or the steps I needed to take to get there. On my father's side of the family, we had relatives who were able to successfully obtain higher education and have thriving careers. I had aunts who were Ivy League graduates. I longed for academic support and mentorship from my own family members, but unfortunately, these relatives went on to be the kind of people who achieved success and looked down on others who hadn't. From then on I was fiercely motivated and knew that if I ever achieved any bit of success, I would always support and mentor others in their journey.

I was blessed to have parents who envisioned for me what they couldn't have for themselves. My parents held me to high standards and always made sure I had all the tools I needed to be successful. They were extremely patient with me, even when I acted out in ways they couldn't understand. Throughout middle school, I struggled with their separation, grappling with new emotions of frustration and disappointment. In constant conflict, I received numerous detentions and suspensions.

For most of my early academic career, I also struggled with ADHD and neurodivergence. It wasn't until I reached seventh grade that I had a history teacher named Ms. Rincon who I felt saw my potential and really pushed me to new heights. She was stern, but had passion and drive to see her students succeed. That year, I went from having straight 75s on my report card to graduating eighth grade on the honor roll. I engaged in community service almost weekly and received a service award at my middle school graduation. Around this time, I started to develop my passion for giving back to my community. Thanks to the confidence Ms. Rincon instilled in me, I remained a dedicated student and achieved straight As all throughout high school. I took AP classes, was on the executive board of clubs, and slowly started to feel confident that I could someday go to college.

ROSE-COLORED GLASSES

When I reached my senior year of high school, I received the exciting news that I would be receiving a full scholarship to a private university. The scholarship would not only fund my education, but would allow me to do social justice work and travel with a cohort of other students during the four year program. The application process involved several writing samples and interviews, and I was selected from over 300 candidates. I remember the overwhelming feelings of joy and pride when I got accepted.

However, when I started school in the fall, the rose-colored glasses immediately came off. I realized I was at a predominantly White institution where I felt lost and like I didn't belong. I struggled to make friends and connect with students outside of my scholarship program. Microaggressions and tone-deaf comments were typical experiences for students of color at this predominantly White institution. I remember one night at a party, a White student asked me, "Are you Indian? Sorry, I just grew up in a town where the only people of color were Indian."

My semester took a turn for the worse when I was sexually assaulted by a classmate in my program. I had to see this person every week in a small class of less than 10 students. This created an internal battle between trying to keep things professional and cordial for the purposes of our class, versus constantly feeling triggered by this person's presence. I remained silent, kept my head down, and tried my best to get through class each week.

THE ROAD TO HEALING

After this traumatic experience, it felt like my world had stopped while everyone else continued to move on around me. I watched as other students enjoyed their college experience, made new friends, and excelled academically—but for me, undergrad felt spoiled and ruined only a few months in. Guilt and shame haunted me everyday. I constantly wondered if it was somehow my fault or if I did something wrong. As I withdrew and isolated myself from others, my grades and academic performance started to decline, to the point where one of my professors shared that she was worried about me. Two months after being sexually assaulted, I found the courage to tell one of my closest friends. I no longer wanted to go through this experience alone, and I grew tired of having forced interactions in class with my assaulter. It felt like a weight was lifted off my shoulders when I finally confided in someone who not only believed me, but also wanted to support me in whatever action I decided to pursue.

After opening up to my friend, I decided to seek professional help from my college's counseling center, where I met with a licensed clinical social worker. The validation and empathy I received from the social worker made me realize that what happened to me was not okay and that it was not my fault. She helped me explore my options and the resources available to me for reporting the incident. Shortly after meeting with her, I found myself starting the reporting process with the university. Meeting with this social worker was extremely helpful to start my healing process. Ultimately, my decision to pursue a career in social work derives from my desire to help other people take back their power in their lives, the way I felt empowered to do that day. In the weeks that followed, I went through the triggering and mentally draining reporting process. Upon finishing, I decided to take a leave for the remainder of the semester and return home. My grades were hanging on by a thread, my focus and motivation were completely nonexistent, and I did not feel like I could give any more of myself to this school.

REDIRECTION

My decision to take some time off from school was met with judgment from relatives. We didn't talk about mental health or trauma in my family, so when I decided to return home to take care of my mental health, it came as a shock. No one knew why, as I was not ready to disclose my experience.

It wasn't until the next fall that I returned to school to complete my undergraduate degree. I decided to enroll at a different university closer to home. For a while, it weighed heavily on me that I took a leave and walked away from a scholarship I worked so hard for. Part of me felt like I had given up by not returning to my scholarship program, but simultaneously I acknowledged that I deserved a fresh start. At my new school, I lived on campus, made a great group of friends, and excelled academically. It was also much more culturally diverse, and I felt a sense of belonging I did not have at my last university.

While there was more diversity, I still experienced microaggressions—this time from my professors. To this day,

I remember the pit in my stomach when my research professor called me out in front of the entire class to say he could tell English was my second language from my most recent writing assignment, as I wasn't as "strong or concise a writer" as other students in the class. The feelings of humiliation and regret for not speaking up for myself haunt me to this day, as my professor continued to single me out as well as other bilingual Latinx-identifying students throughout the semester. After three years of persevering, I went on to graduate with my Bachelors of Arts in Psychology in May 2020 and immediately enrolled in my Masters in Social Work program the following fall.

REFLECTION: STRENGTH IN VULNERABILITY

Looking back at my undergraduate experience, I often wish I could reassure my younger self that taking time away from school was not the equivalent to giving up or failing—it was a matter of taking care of my mental health. I was unable to be my best self during my first semester of college, as I was operating in survival mode after a deeply traumatic event. In my early academic years, I validated myself a lot through my academic performance and work ethic. My self-worth was so deeply entrenched in how well I could perform, how much I could take on at once, and how many accomplishments I could achieve.

I now give myself grace for the ways I chose to heal, which required embracing new beginnings. I applaud myself for no longer allowing school and academics to dictate my worth. My leave of absence was the first time I learned that taking care of yourself is necessary in your academic and professional endeavors, a lesson that would become essential for someone pursuing a career in social work. This experience also taught me that you don't have to push yourself to operate in survival mode—it is more than okay to honor your limits and take a step back.

Latina women are often expected to be strong and bear our trauma without portraying "weakness." We are taught to be grateful for what we have. We are constantly reminded that those who came before us "had it worse." We face an immeasurable amount of pressure to handle everything that comes our way with grace. However, this experience taught me that everyone has different ways of dealing with their trauma and grief, and that we should not normalize or minimize our suffering.

All my life, I thought strength was the ability to navigate challenges and trauma without showing any sign of weakness. I have since learned that there is strength in facing your trauma head-on, even when it involves taking time off or starting over. I am glad that I embraced redirection, rather than running from it. By taking a break and prioritizing my well-being, I was able to return to my education with a renewed focus and passion. This redirection led me to a university where I made amazing friends and felt seen and comfortable in my identity. Being redirected also led to me becoming a Masters in Social Work graduate from Fordham University, and becoming a Licensed Psychotherapist in group private practice. I hope my story serves as a reminder that sometimes our perceived setbacks are actually blessings in disguise. Like an arrow, sometimes we need to move backwards in order to be propelled forward to reach greater heights.

Thank you to my Madrina Dr. Jessica Hardial for sponsoring and mentoring me.

Ancestral Wisdom:

From my Grandmother Altagracia: Dios nunca llega tarde. (God never arrives late.)

Journal Prompts:

1. What is one way that you have prioritized taking care of your mental, emotional, and spiritual well-being recently?
2. Looking back, what setbacks in your life now seem like blessings in disguise?

BIOGRAPHY

Natalie Gutierrez, LMSW is a licensed psychotherapist specializing in trauma, CPTSD, grief, anxiety, BIPOC individuals and LGBTQIA+ communities. She serves as Program Coordinator for Emotions Matter, a nonprofit dedicated to providing advocacy and support to individuals living with Borderline Personality Disorder. Natalie is also the host of her own podcast called "Tea Time" where she has conversations with other professionals in the mental health and social work fields. Natalie proudly identifies as Dominican-American.

Natalie received her Masters in Social Work from Fordham University Graduate School of Social Services and her Bachelors of Arts in Psychology from SUNY College at Old Westbury. Natalie is a current doctoral student at the University of Kentucky's Doctorate of Social Work Program.

JARAN DAVID MANZANET, MSW

"I've learned that social work is not about proving to others what you can do, but rather understanding your limits and becoming aware of your strengths."

THE IN-BETWEEN

As a second-generation Latino and eldest son, I have constantly found myself negotiating the in-between. The in-between of my parents not teaching me Spanish but hoping my grandmother would. The in-between of becoming a de facto third parent as I helped to raise my three younger siblings, born more than a decade after I was. The in-between of benefitting from male privilege while the world also treats me as a minority. The in-between of my family expecting the best from me while the world expects the worst.

Mama—the name for my maternal grandmother—told me the world was a big place, and I could be Mayor Manzanet because I had a smile that would light up any room and ease anyone's pain. But that's not how the world saw me. At age 12, the police called me racial slurs and told me that gang violence would kill me by age 16 or that if I made it to 21, I'd have five kids and be stabbed to death.

My career choice is a result of this dual experience. The oppression other Latinx/e individuals and I faced made me want to fight for a better world, and Mama made me believe I could. The negative Puerto Rican stereotypes that flood the world made me want to push against the false narratives, tell my story, speak up for Latinos who fight these narratives on a daily basis, and take pride in knowing we are strong, resilient people. I've always had a deep connection to our people, my ancestors, even if I could never really explain it. Their blood courses through me and so does their trauma, and both propelled me into social work. I wanted to fight for those who seemed voiceless because I too often felt voiceless.

I felt voiceless at home, where I was the eldest of four and often felt unheard. I now understand my parents did the best they could. They were in college when they had me, and even though they had a very large support system, I got lost in the shuffle at times. I know they weren't trying to ignore me, but it was the cost of them trying to figure it all out.

Experiences with my name also made me feel unheard. For years, I allowed white people to say it however they saw fit. It fascinated me how white people would try twice and then just tell me how they were going to say my name. I would give up after they failed to get it right. It was frustrating, overwhelming, and annoying at minimum. My parents understood, but they didn't listen to how much it bothered me. So in high school, I started going by the nickname JD, which was what my mother and my mother alone called me. When she found out I had the whole school calling me JD, she was livid to say the least. She felt betrayed. Yet we never had a sit-down about how it made us feel. Just like many other issues, it was swept under the rug and avoided. The next day, everything went back to normal.

It wasn't until I started social work school that I wanted to go by my full name: Jaran David Manzanet. I wanted to reclaim that power, have a better understanding of why I should be respected by my peers, and make sure they said my name the way it was meant to be said. I wanted to remind people I am not the third, or a junior, that I have a first and middle name, and you will address me by both since it is my name. "I came in without an ordinary name," my favorite rapper, Nas, once said. This is true—I came in without an ordinary name. There's something in a name that's different from theirs.

Finding my way back to my name also led me back to my Spanish. Even though I grew up knowing that both my parents could speak Spanish, they didn't speak it with me. They were concentrated on assimilating and conforming to American culture. My mother was also self-conscious of her Spanish ability, so she relied on Mama, her mother, to speak to me in Spanish. But taking a cue from my parents about assimilation,

I only replied to Mama in English. As a child I hid from the opportunity to expand my linguistic abilities because I thought it was good to hide from the world. But I also felt less than other Latinos who were fluent in Spanish—I was living the in-between of knowing some Spanish while not being fluent in it. All I ever wanted was to be part of a larger community, just like my large family comes together and makes us feel like we all belong. I believe this is where my rebellious spirit comes from. I now refuse to code switch in many spaces because how I speak shows people authentically where I am from and how I want to be presented.

I am not where I want to be with my Spanish just yet, though I am proud to be shedding my Latino imposter syndrome thanks to this newfound path. I understand that Spanish is the oppressor's language (shoutout to Antonio Morales, LCSW for teaching me this history). Yet Spanish is embedded in our DNA now, and we should try to feel a connection to it to a degree. Working on it is a journey to a bigger goal: showcasing that I'm not willing to conform to certain societal viewpoints and won't be burdened by expectations and stereotypes of what a Puerto Rican from the Bronx (a Nuyorican!) "should be."

ATLAS

Living in the in-between has meant that it's not enough to just be a good son and brother. I also need to not be a failure so that my siblings can look up to me. I have to make everyone proud of me because it is my job as a Manzanet to live up to what others have done. No one asked me if it was hard; they just said I had to succeed. The mounting pressure to do well in school, while trying to help my parents with the kids, led to fatigue in college. I know now that it was more than just fatigue. It was a burnout. I had a goal of making sure I graduated "on time," yet was also working so that I wasn't a financial burden to my parents. I took my siblings to and from school and helped them with their homework while also trying to finish my own projects, inevitably sacrificing my social life. This, coupled with a relationship that pushed me to the brink mentally, made me turn to sleeping pills to get some rest, which almost killed me.

I was on the phone with a friend venting about my struggles while taking the pills and just passed out. It was 16 hours later when I regained consciousness. Yet no one said anything. My parents seemed oblivious to it. It was the most extreme example of how I ran away from my problems, not knowing how to grieve, thinking I could handle everything without anyone's help. If I could survive this, I could finish school and be the example everyone wanted me to be.

In retrospect, anxiety was kicking my butt left and right. I didn't feel like I had anyone to speak to about these expectations of a second-generation Latino who was also the eldest. Setting the stage for future generations was a burden, which is why I chose the pen name Atlas—I was presented with the challenge of balancing the heavens on my shoulders and proving to everyone that I could achieve everything that was put in front of me. I've learned that social work is not about proving to others what you can do, but rather understanding your limits and becoming aware of your strengths. By coming to these realizations at the end of the day, it leads me to a line from the rapper Nas, "The sun doesn't even know it's a star!"

Thank you to my padrino Cristino Chavez for your sponsorship and guidance.

Ancestral Wisdom:

Say your whole name, so your ancestors live on. Your name is powerful, you are powerful.

Journal Prompts:

1. What are some ways you have assimilated to make others feel more comfortable?
2. What does your mental health journey look like? Can you identify your safe space, and are you allowing yourself the opportunity to heal?

BIOGRAPHY

Jaran David Manzanet, MSW was raised in The Bronx and is now a resident of Harlem. He works as a Functional Family Therapist, helping youths between the ages of 11-18 build support systems with family members and their communities. He has been in social service since 2014 and has worked on Community Board projects for Harlem's District 10. Currently awaiting to retake the License Exam at the time of publication, Jaran David is also deciding on the best options for continuing education in the field of social work.

SUFRÍ, APRENDÍ, CAMBIÉ

VIVIANNA MORFIN, ASW

---

*"Tanto sufrimiento que pasamos ni cómo saber
en dónde empezar."*

Nina, this one is for you. I love you and miss you so much.

SUFRÍ

"Tanto sufrimiento que pasamos ni cómo saber en dónde empezar," my grandma Victoria said as we sat on the porch outside our house in Ukiah, telling my brother and I about her journey from Mexico to the United States. She was born and raised in a small town in Jalisco, Mexico, called San Nicolas de Ibarra. This is where she met my grandpa Salvador. They got married when my grandma was just 18 years old, and had five children within 10 years. One of those children was my mom.

On February 4, 1982, their worlds changed forever when my grandpa took his own life. After this tragic event, my grandma felt like she was left with no choice but to migrate to the United States in hopes of giving her family a better life. On March 7 of that same year, when my mom was just eight years old, she and her family made the long, difficult journey to the United States. They were separated throughout the process, but were luckily all reunited when they made it to San Francisco. If it wasn't for the risk that my grandma had taken that day 40 years ago, I would not be here, on the balcony of my mom's house in Mexico, writing this chapter today.

I grew up in a single parent household and was raised by the most amazing woman that I know. Mami, I love you and admire you so much! My dad left when I was five, and his absence created a void in me and made life a lot harder than it should have been. Everyone thought all my sadness came from my dad leaving, but there was so much more causing me pain at that age. My mother suffered so much during this time, and as her hurt turned into anger, she took me with her through the whole journey. I was a daddy's girl at heart, so him leaving our family to start another family, and watching the two people I loved the most grow to hate each other, tore me apart. I didn't understand why he was leaving us. I didn't understand why I was helping my mom cut up her wedding dress. Thoughts like, *"Why am I not good enough? What did I do wrong? What did I do to deserve this? Why doesn't he love me? How can I help my mom and dad stay together?"* ran through my head every day. It wasn't until I was 21 that I was able to come to terms with his abandonment and not feel like it was my fault or that I could have prevented it.

After three very long, challenging years of moving around due to the financial difficulties of living on a single income, my mom decided to open a restaurant with my aunt—a very successful restaurant that has been open since September 30, 2005, and is now solely owned by my mother. When my mom was opening this restaurant, she was still working full time at a hardware store. Between a full-time job and being a business owner, she spent a lot of time away from home. Most days, she got ready for work at 5 a.m. and wouldn't return until 9 p.m., which meant that I was now the one in charge of keeping things together at home. This entailed getting my brother ready for preschool, keeping the house clean, feeding the dog, finishing homework, and taking care of myself, all at eight years old. Part of me felt so proud and honored that she trusted me enough to get all these things done, but the other part wanted my mom home and for someone to take care of me.

Looking after my brother gave me a purpose. He was my reason to keep going and motivated me to want to be better. Whenever I felt like giving up, I would think about how Alex needed me. He was my partner in crime, someone I could laugh with, cry with, and feel safe with. Alex has been a constant safe presence in my life; he is the one man who has stayed, and never left or hurt me.

What I went through at a young age made me very vulnerable and desperate for attachment. As a child, I had a hole in me that needed to be filled. Over time, I thought I was filling that emptiness. A part of me was happy that I was finally able to find love and connection, or what I thought those things felt and looked like. But at six years old, how was I supposed to understand that people will take advantage of you? That at six years old, no one should be putting their hands on your temple? That at six years old, you have a voice? I felt like I didn't have a voice. Everyone was so busy doing other things, I felt like no one had time for me, no one would love me, and no one would believe me.

It wasn't until I was much older in high school that I realized what six-year-old me went through wasn't love, connection, or attachment. There I was, yet again, asking myself the same questions as when my dad left: *"What did I do wrong? What did I do to deserve this?"* I later realized it was a violation of the worst kind, to prey on a vulnerable child. It was abuse, it was someone taking advantage of me, it was someone who didn't love me, and it wasn't my fault.

APRENDÍ

My mom always wanted the best for my brother and me. She had the same response every time I asked her why she worked so much: "I want the best para ti y Alex, Vivianna." It didn't make sense to me then, but I understand her now. With everything that she, her siblings, and my grandma went through when she was growing up, she felt like she had to be the absolute best that she could. I know this because it's how I feel about my own journey and giving back to my mom.

This quest for perfection can be a blessing and a curse. Since she wanted the best for us, my mom sent us to a private Catholic school. Even though she could not afford to pay tuition out of pocket like most of the other parents, she did what she needed to get us there. I remember showing up on the first day of school at the start of second grade. I looked around and could count on both hands how many brown and black students there were in the whole school. I didn't want to be there; I felt uncomfortable and wanted to go home. At that moment, this little girl came up to me with her mom. My skin was beautifully brown and rich like chocolate, whereas hers was beautifully light and radiant like a diamond. Our moms introduced themselves to each other, and apparently it was both of our first days. Still very shy and embarrassed, I introduced myself. Little did I know that Ashlynn would be my Godsent angel for life.

Walking into that private Catholic school was the first time I really felt and noticed racism and discrimination, but it wasn't my last. I have experienced microaggressions many times throughout my educational and professional career, and they never stop feeling like little stabs. It wasn't until I learned what a microaggression was that I realized I had been experiencing them even within my own family. I remember hearing statements from relatives all the time like, "You're too dark to wear that color. You need to scrub yourself harder in the shower. You can't be that princess for Halloween because you're too dark. You must have been adopted." Comments that everyone thought were funny, but deep inside made me feel like I was never good enough. These statements prompted me to dye my hair blond, avoid being in the sun, and hate the colors yellow and orange because they highlighted my darker skin tones.

It wasn't until I moved to Florida in 2018 and felt like I fit in with the diverse Latino and Caribbean population that I was able to fully accept myself. I now take so much pride in the color of my skin and love myself exactly the way that I am, beautifully brown and rich like chocolate.

CAMBIÉ

Being a first-generation Mexican American comes with many different obstacles. If you add that to also being a first-generation college student and graduate, it almost seems impossible. But I am a living testimony que sí se puede.

In 2017, I was attending Sonoma State on track to receive my bachelor's in business administration with a concentration in management. I desperately needed a job since my family couldn't afford to pay my tuition. Part of me was also embarrassed to ever ask my mom for money since she had already sacrificed so much for me to get to where I was. My cousin helped me get a job at the Boys and Girls Club, and even though I was extremely grateful for the opportunity, I was not sure that I wanted to work with kids. In desperate need, I took the job anyway. I was placed as a program coordinator in a low-income Latino-populated area in Santa Rosa working with at-risk teens.

After a week on the job, I knew this was what I was meant to do. I didn't know what the work was called or if there were careers in this field, but I knew I wanted to help people and give back to the community. It felt like home, and I was transformed in a profound way. My supervisor Katie helped me grow both professionally and personally at the organization. She encouraged, pushed, and motivated me to be the best version of myself. Katie helped me see how bright my future is in this field that I now know as social work.

During my senior year, I went through a deep depression after my first breakup. I did not feel good enough for anyone or anything, which caused me to skip classes and give up on school. When I finished my degree, I had a 2.6 GPA. Thankfully, there was still a small spark in me that shone through and I was able to graduate. But when I thought about grad school, I was extremely nervous and lacked confidence in myself, my work, and my grades.

I started grad school applications in 2020. I applied to two Master of Social Work programs, San Jose State and Sacramento State. A few months later, I received letters from both schools. I remember seeing the first line, "We regret to inform you that…" and stopped reading. Once again, I was not good enough. I wasn't a right fit. I thought that maybe grad school wasn't for people like me.

I felt like no one understood what I was going through, but there was one person who did. Even though we came from different cultures, races, and backgrounds, she got me, and I got her. Stephanie, an extraordinary social worker who I now have the honor of calling my Tía, pushed me to keep trying. She said that this field needed more people like me and that I would find the right program that would accept me for me. I just needed to keep looking.

In 2021, I decided to reapply for grad school, but this time I looked at MSW programs out of state. I applied to four different schools, but there was one I preferred over the others. On October 1, 2021, when I was in Saint Thomas celebrating my birthday, I received a call from my top choice, Fordham University, notifying me that I had been accepted into their accelerated track MSW program. In that moment, I knew my life would change forever and that the generational trauma that my family had suffered for years would be closer to ending because of me. It has been a long road coming, but I have made it.

Thank you to Laudy Burgos, my madrina in social work, for sponsoring and mentoring me. The knowledge and love that you shared with me throughout this experience is something I will hold onto forever. Thank you for helping me ease into the medical social work field and see that I am more than capable of being a hospital social worker.

Ancestral Wisdom:

"You don't take your money with you when you die—you have to live now."

Journal Prompts:
1. Whose cultural definitions and expectations are you living by?
2. What do your culture's traditional values cost you? How do they serve you?
3. What makes you feel safe? Who is your "safe person?"

BIOGRAPHY

Vivianna Morfin, ASW works as an inpatient social worker for the OB, ICU, and ER at a hospital in the rural town of Ukiah, California. Prior to entering the medical social work field, she worked as a mental health clinician providing therapeutic services in English and Spanish to families with limited resources. Vivianna also started an annual Toy and Food holiday fundraiser in her mother's hometown of San Nicolás de Ibarra in Jalisco, Mexico. She is an alumnus from Fordham University's graduate school of social service and recipient of the 2023 Future of Social Work award from the Latino Social Work Coalition. Vivianna hopes to use her degrees in business management and social work to help BIPOC communities reach their greatest potential.

SIEMPRE ES POSIBLE: LEADERSHIP AS AN ECOSYSTEM OF COMPASSIONATE GROWTH

DR. JUAN A. RIOS, DSW, LCSW

"La lucha no es fácil, pero siempre es posible."
—Omar Torrijos Herrera

EL CAMINO (THE JOURNEY)

My social work journey started in the busy streets of New Haven, Connecticut. It was one of the first battlegrounds where my family would eventually learn to demonstrate our resilience. A short walk away was a local soup kitchen where we would spend every Thursday evening having dinner. The best part of that dinner was the end. Why? Yup, Boston Crème Donuts. I would wait through the dry rye bread that could choke a dinosaur, mashed potatoes that needed the entire Dead Sea to season them, and hard frozen peas that by the end of the night we used as table weapons. But finally, our hero, a slinky hipster with a large black garbage bag around his shoulder, would heave the bag of discarded donuts to the middle of the floor and poof! We instantly transformed into Mad Max characters. In that bag was pure joy—Boston Crème Donuts. We stuffed our faces and pockets to the brim.

We could not wait to walk back home and share our treats with our friends. We lived in a vibrant, thriving community where we played games in the streets until the lights came on, sharing Honeybuns and Boston Crèmes. I can still remember the handlebar mustache of the bodega owner who would give my mother credit for food when we were low on groceries. Here, credit was not based on scores, but rather trust.

Our brick apartment building was only two blocks away from a prestigious institution of higher education—Yale. But my home felt hundreds of miles away from the University. Campus police would be ready to make sure to let the neighborhood kids know which side of the street belonged to the community and which side belonged to the University. On one side, we would see twill jackets with leather patches; on the other, a playground filled with broken crack vials.

The displacement our family experienced as Yale University grew was a powerful indicator of the larger forces at work to keep us at bay. When I was eight, I sat on the cold stoop with my sister, watching our clothes, toys, and entire life be stuffed into a rusted moving truck, our things in large garbage bags. One by one, black trash bag after black trash bag was carried out like a factory line, stretching from our apartment to the streets. I hid my face in my sweater to hide my tears. Our neighbors watched from their windows and porches in grief; it was almost like being at your own wake. It was a gut-wrenching feeling that nothing would ever be the same.

The University was making way for faculty housing. Our block was purchased, and we were evicted. No, we were discarded. It was not a choice; it was a decision. A decision made by those who had the power to design a new community that did not include us. No discussion, no relocation assistance, no more playing tag in the streets with friends, no more evening dinners down the street or Boston Crème Donuts, no more bodega credit. My world ended as our lives changed forever.

New Haven, CT, is the classic tale of two cities: poverty disparity alongside institutions housed in underserved communities that literally change landscapes from one side of the street to the other. There is Yale, and there is New Haven.

This was one of my very first experiences with institutions of higher education, and it was not the only moment in my life where I witnessed oppressive power. I have seen systems, policies, and initiatives be designed that excluded at-risk populations like my mother who lives with schizophrenia, my brother who spent most of his life in the justice system, and my friends who lost their lives to gun violence.

At an early age, I felt a burn within that I needed to do

something. This is where my leadership was born. My experiences have shaped my dedication to being a voice for those who often go unheard. I became a social worker to advocate for those left out of decision rooms and to be a champion for those who carried their lives in black trash bags.

As a faculty professor at another institution of higher education, every single time I step on campus, I arrive in a state of dual consciousness where my lived experience of loss and displacement meets my reality of working for an institution that also has its own history of community accountability. It gets hard, real hard.

The only way I realized how to exist in this state of dual consciousness is to dedicate my work to community-engaged scholarship. Engaged Scholarship, a term coined by Andrew Van de Ven, refers to an approach to research that actively involves academics, community members, and practitioners in collaborative long-term partnerships that address real-world problems.

My experiences gave fuel to that fire inside of me. When I started out as a social worker, my idealism was rooted in the injustices that had marked my own childhood. This created a very shaky relationship, where I was looking to root myself in community accountability while having lived an academic life for nearly nine years. But, at the end of it all, this is also why I made a commitment to integrate community-engaged scholarship into work and change oppressive systems. I began to see that the path of a social worker is everywhere—not just meeting short-term needs, but also working towards long-lasting changes in society with kindness.

TRAUMATIC TRANSFERENCE AND PERSONAL GROWTH

The work shows up and shows me something

On a brisk fall afternoon, I met Maria, a young undocumented Latina woman who had endured severe trauma. Her story was one of overcoming impossible odds. At 15, she claimed asylum at the border. At 22, she was now left with psychological trauma from her voyage and lived in constant anxiety of deportation. Maria's healing journey required empathy and an appreciation of what it's like to be undocumented in America, which lots of therapy does not usually support in full. Maria began to heal through our work together. When I say together, I mean we both had healing to do. As she kept healing and improving, she inspired others in her community to seek help, illustrating the ripple effect of compassionate leadership.

Many Latinx social workers have less accessible routes into the field. Our challenges are often linked to issues of race, xenophobia and ethnicity, not to mention systemic bias, cultural misunderstandings, and resource constraints. Resilience is crucial in the face of these challenges. Where we are from, our cultural relevance, helps form us professionally. Triumphs in social work often look like small successes, marked by many challenges, but which add up to something great.

EMBRACING AN ECOSYSTEM OF CARE

Latinx culture is recognized as a vital component to improving social work practice. Cultural competence is more than we often talk about; it goes deep to a respectful state of understanding our client's story and how they look at the world. In practice, that may mean listening to our clients' narratives with new ears, recognizing their hidden cultural resources, and incorporating them in our interventions. For example, traditional healing practices and community rituals can be used as therapeutic interventions. We pay homage to the cultural roots of our clients and expand our professional universe with indigenous perspectives, values, and methods.

Compassionate leadership in social work is not simply being a case manager; it requires advocacy and systemic change. A few characteristics of compassionate leaders include empathy, expertise in human resilience, and the ability to appreciate other cultures as well as a strong inclination towards justice. As social workers, advocating for our communities is a fundamental part of the job and systemically speaking there are many factors disproportionately burdening Latino/a/x folks by their very existence. Effective advocacy strategies include forming coalitions with community members, utilizing data to identify disparities, and influencing policy at a systems level.

HARNESSING TRAUMA AS A PLATFORM FOR WELL-BEING AND RADICAL MOTION TOWARDS JUSTICE

Although trauma can be crippling, one of its other facets is growth and evolution. Social workers can play an integral role in facilitating individual and communal healing, leveraging the trauma as a gateway toward all things positive. Within the realm of social work practice are a number of steps to integrating compassionate leadership and emergent strategy in an organization:

1. **Engaging Communities:** Participate in community members in all facets, design through implementation. Their experiences and perspectives are invaluable in developing solutions that work and last.

2. **Collaborative Leadership:** Build a culture of collaboration and collective leadership. Empower community members to lead initiatives and grow in leadership.

3. **Adaptive Approaches:** Adjust your approach to meet shifting needs and circumstances. Use feedback and insights in order to adapt interventions where necessary or discuss new strategies with decision-makers.

4. **Prioritizing Healing:** Make healing and well-being the center focus in all aspects of social work. Understanding trauma and responding to both immediate needs and recovery as Nicotera (2020) described.

Through the weaving of personal stories with notions of compassionate leadership, which are informed by emergent strategy, we can bring them into and inspire a more holistic approach to social work towards our collective thriving. When valid, trauma—when recognized and addressed with compassion—can be a source of healing for both the individual and community, setting us on paths to establishing new norms toward an equitable society.

Mentorship in social work transcends the traditional role of merely transferring knowledge; it involves cultivating a shared vision for social justice and community empowerment. This journey is particularly critical for Latinx social workers, who often navigate unique challenges tied to systemic inequalities and cultural dynamics (Fong et al., 2016). These challenges demand a compassionate, culturally attuned form of leadership—one that is rooted in empathy and resilience, qualities that are integral to the practice of social work.

In the broader context of social work, mentorship becomes a vital tool for transforming individual experiences into collective wisdom. When seasoned social workers share their stories of resilience and growth, they ignite a ripple effect that not only inspires the next generation but also contributes to the ongoing evolution of the profession. This exchange fosters a deeper sense of cultural competency and inclusivity, enhancing the quality of care provided to communities (Ortega-Williams et al., 2021).

Emergent strategies play a crucial role in these mentoring relationships. By fostering open dialogue and encouraging collaborative problem-solving, mentors and mentees can co-create innovative approaches to addressing complex social issues. This approach aligns perfectly with adrienne maree brown's framework of emergent strategy, which emphasizes adaptability and responsiveness to real-world challenges. In this framework, change is seen as an ongoing, interconnected process—one that empowers communities to take ownership of their health and well-being (Rios et al., 2018).

The significance of mentoring in trauma-informed care cannot be understated. Mentors who have navigated their own experiences of trauma offer invaluable support to those facing similar challenges, creating a safe and supportive environment where mentees can develop resilience. This shared understanding allows for the kind of healing that is both personal and professional, ultimately enhancing the ability to provide compassionate care to clients (Knight, 2018).

To fully harness the transformative power of mentoring in social work, we must integrate the following concepts:

1. **Cultural Humility:** Encourage mentors to engage with their mentees' diverse experiences openly. This reciprocal learning process fosters a more inclusive and equitable mentoring relationship.

2. **Trauma-Informed Mentoring:** Embed trauma-informed principles into mentoring practices to create a supportive environment for professional growth.

This approach acknowledges the profound impact of personal and collective trauma on professional development.

3. **Community-Centered Mentoring:** Expand the scope of mentoring beyond individual relationships to include community engagement and collective learning. This aligns with the principles of engaged scholarship, promoting a shared responsibility for community well-being.

By embracing mentorship as an integral part of social work, we create an ecosystem of compassionate growth—an ecosystem that nurtures emerging leaders, strengthens community bonds, and contributes to the collective healing of the communities we serve. Mentorship becomes not just a tool for knowledge transfer but a catalyst for social justice, igniting the passion that drives our profession forward.

In the words of Omar Torrijos Herrera, "La lucha no es fácil, pero siempre es posible." Through mentorship, we reaffirm that while the struggle for justice and equity is not easy, it is always possible when we uplift one another. Mentorship in social work creates a legacy of compassionate leadership—one that extends far beyond individual careers, shaping the future of the profession and the communities we serve for generations to come.

This work is not easy or achieved quickly, as we know that the journey of a social worker will be challenged and tested to its very limits—but with compassion, resilience, and an unwavering commitment towards our collective well-being, perhaps then together we can start making real care reform that embraces all of who are, how we show up, and how we are now choosing to co-design our communities we want to live in.

Journal Prompts:

1. Do you have your own example of collaborative leadership?
2. What does your personal healing journey look like, and how has it helped your growth?
3. Who are some of your mentors? How have they supported you personally and/or professionally?

BIOGRAPHY

Dr. Juan A. Rios Jr., an Associate Professor at Seton Hall University, is a first-generation college graduate dedicated to social justice and community well-being. With over two decades of clinical and academic experience, he champions liberation health models, mindfulness practices, and transformative education. He founded the RIOS Lab, pioneering research in social justice and technology, including empathy-building through virtual reality. Recognized for his innovative teaching and community-based participatory research, Dr. Rios bridges disciplines to reduce health disparities among marginalized communities. His life's work centers on empowering the underrepresented, fostering compassionate communities, and integrating cutting-edge solutions with holistic, community-engaged scholarship.

References:

- Brown, a. m. (2017). Emergent strategy: Shaping change, changing worlds. AK Press.
- Fong, R., Dettlaff, A. J., James, J., & Rodriguez, C. (2016). *Addressing racial disproportionality and disparities in human services: Multisystemic approaches.* Columbia University Press.
- Knight, C. (2018). Trauma-informed supervision in social work. *The Clinical Supervisor,* 37(1), 7-21.
- Nicotera, A. (2020). Circle of insight: A paradigm and process for applied social research. *Journal of Social Work Education,* 56(3), 492-506.
- Ortega-Williams, A., Crutchfield, J., & Hall, J. C. (2021). The colorist-historical trauma framework: Implications for culturally responsive practice with African Americans. *Journal of Social Work*, 21(3), 294-309.
- Rios, Juan (2022). "Teaching Note: Bridging Contemplative Social Work Education and Emerging Technologies," *Journal of Contemplative Inquiry:* Vol. 9: No. 1, Article 20.

Our Roots:

Identity, an Internal and External Struggle

———

ZULEYKA AYALA, LMSW

"Something lit up in me, and I felt an inner nudge to self-advocate my way through this birth and manifest it to myself, que sí se puede…"

UNPLANNED: NOT ALONE CAPRICORN

As the wind whipped and the snow came down in torrents, I waddled to catch the D train to the 1 train to my destination: the labor and delivery department of NewYork-Presbyterian Allen Pavilion for my scheduled induced labor. At the time, I was staying with my parents in the South Bronx, the same apartment my grandparents migrated to from Honduras. It felt surreal being in the same apartment where my mother lived during her teens and where my grandparents became caretakers of me and my older sibling while my parents worked the 3-11 p.m. shift at a factory in Queens. This apartment became both a safe haven and a place of undesirably built resiliency.

That resiliency was embedded in me as I traveled to the hospital in one of the worst blizzards in New York City's history, a snowstorm that brought the city to a standstill with over 30 inches of snow in the span of two days. But the winter advisory didn't hold me back from taking public transit and then walking all the way to the hospital with my mother and older sibling in tow. My family questioned me during the entire journey leading up to Eladius' birth, wondering if I should be traversing the blizzard while pregnant and overdue. That's when I told myself, *"Atrévete"* (dare yourself).

The questioning continued when we got to the hospital, the medical team skeptical that I was fully dilated and ready to push and not just feeling an oncoming bowel movement from the *chuletas fritas con moro y ensalada* I had my mother make earlier that night. As a daring child entering her young adulthood having a child of her own, I knew when I was ready to push! My mother's stories about her experiences giving birth started to flood my mind. I recalled how she told me she'd felt out of control, unheard, and unseen. Something lit up in me, and I felt an inner nudge to self-advocate my way through this birth and manifest it to myself, *que sí se puede!* Subconsciously, I had the need to prove to my family and then mother-in-law that I was going to thrive in pushing my first-born son without being your lowkey *pendeja*!

Giving birth to Eladius was not only a selfless act, but it

was also the turning point of what self-sacrifice meant to me. At a very young age, I learned the importance of self-sacrifice in helping build the foundation of a home. But while giving birth, I began to question my own experiences as a child and realized the importance of creating a secure attachment with my own kid. I initially thought that being pregnant was a huge decision, but in actuality, moving out of my parents' home to live in a basement makeshift studio apartment was the icing on the cake. Not only did I move out with my son, but I moved to the other side of the Bronx, a decision that led to guilt and pain due to the unknown of what life outside of my childhood stomping grounds would look like.

INDECISION ROADMAP

I started to recognize what loneliness felt and looked like. It began to hit me in waves when I held onto Eladius. I would catch myself caressing his forehead and his nose as he drifted off to sleep. I had these overwhelming feelings that were indescribable but very real. I started to have flashbacks and reintegrated memories in areas that had been hidden until then. Much of my reflection happened in this time period. I began to journal and meditate about my lived experiences with my elders, photographs of my past, and how giving birth to a boy was a true testament of who I would end up becoming—a Latina social worker from the South Bronx.

Prior to becoming pregnant with Eladius, I was an undergraduate student at New York City College of Technology after transferring from SUNY Canton. Honestly, I couldn't find my niche, but I was invested in getting some sort of college degree as a first-generation Latina. At that time, I was majoring in liberal arts with a minor in African American studies. Less than a year after Eladius was born, I transferred again, this time to the social work department at Lehman College. However, I ended up on academic probation; I couldn't balance being a parent to a newborn, a student, a daughter, an employee, and a partner. I was struggling, and instead of seeking help, I withdrew. I began to hear others' voices in my head: how inadequate I was, how I ruined my life, how I wouldn't amount to anything. My mind was bombarded with the negative self-talk I had inherited since childhood from witnessing women in my family be self-critical of their bodies, their abilities, their contributions, their trauma, and their lack of support.

Retrieving my Lehman transcript and staring at the line of Ws that indicated my probation warning, I suddenly felt my knees hit the ground as tears streamed down my face. My heart was racing, my hands were trembling as if it were 0 degrees, I began to rock myself back and forth, and I gripped my chest due to extreme pains. And that's when it hit me: I had seen both my mother and older sibling also collapse in such disbelief and pain due to their own experiences. I finally recognized the symptoms of a panic attack and discovered the generational traumas within our family.

¡QUE CHIVO CIPOTA!

I started to become aware of the generational abuse that women in our family tree had gone through. It was like Tetris—my form of alignment in understanding the missed opportunities in psychosocial development, the patterns of complex post-traumatic stress disorder, anxiety, depression, dissociation, low self-esteem, and distorted body-image. The women were the foundational pillars of their families, yet the women were "damaged goods" when standing next to the man. The pivotal moment in my life came when I started to recognize the self-sacrificing steps my mother and older sibling had taken when they became mothers. I became upset at how we continued generational cycles of self-abandonment.

This aha moment matters because it led to building a family in a way that was healing instead of self-sacrificing. I was given the opportunity to be a mother and give life to a baby who now proudly identifies as a Latino. I was given the chance to persevere through and learn how to unconditionally love someone male. Why does this matter? At seven years old I was sexually abused, which I now know is all too common an experience for women and girls. I had to shift my anger about men into a space of healing. That's when I decided to work full-time and start my journey in the human services profession. This newfound love and joy were explored further and handled with care as I began to learn about trauma, parenting styles, attachment styles, and substance use.

That's when I knew I had to re-enroll in school. I reapplied, got accepted, and graduated with honors from New York City College of Technology. Through this huge educational discovery, I developed skills in empathy and compassion, and finally accepted what I could and could not control. This journey led me to become the social worker and mother I am today. I've learned to always speak the loudest in a room full of naysayers and to be the one to welcome the next person willing to sit at the table. If there is one thing I have learned over the years of service, it's that you don't have to do it alone.

Thank you to my Madrina Cristina Contreras for sponsoring me, and to all the authors before me who have inspired me.

Ancestral Wisdom:

No te resbales, sigue adelante.

Journal Prompts:

1. What patterns and behaviors have you witnessed between men and women in your family, and how has this impacted your life?

2. What steps have you taken to foster secure relationships with your family?

3. Have you ever had an aha moment? What was it?

BIOGRAPHY

Zuleyka Ayala, LMSW, is a dedicated school social worker and bilingual mental health therapist serving individuals and families across New York City. As the founder of AtréveteNow and a mother to her son, Eladius, Zuleyka has a strong personal and professional commitment to her community. She is contracted by Inspiring Futures, a grassroots organization, to continue providing mental health services to youth and young adults with current or past foster care, kinship, or adoption history. Zuleyka earned her MSW from Fordham University in May 2021 and is currently an aspiring LCSW and a Doctorate of Social Work Candidate at LIU, Brooklyn Campus.

LinkedIn: http://linkedin.com/in/ayalaz08
Email: Ayala.TherapyVibez@gmail.com
Social Media: AtreveteNow

THIS IS A WORK IN PROGRESS...

MICHELLE CASTILLO, LCSW

"Our healing does not need to be linear or prescriptive or exacting. It doesn't always need to involve a specific everyday practice (even though it definitely helps!). There just needs to be a gentle reminder to do the things that help bring you back to center and a process to continue figuring out what those things are."

MY INHERITANCE

Like many Latinx/e social workers, the signs were there early on that this was my calling. I inherited my sense of compassion and self-sacrifice like gifts passed down from previous generations. My parents came from close-knit families that were *bondadoso*—charitable. My mother tells stories of her childhood living in La Torre, un campo de La Vega, where everyone knew each other. When any traveler passed through, the villagers gave them food and a place to stay. And after she came to America, my paternal grandmother opened her home to other family members when they immigrated.

In my childhood home, I was taught that if someone knocks on your door, you offer them a plate of food, even if you only made enough for yourself. By the time I was five I knew that our old clothes would be donated. We always picked a tag off the church Christmas tree, letting us know what to buy for a child who was less fortunate. I volunteered with family at soup kitchens, and I started contributing more to the box of canned goods we collected and kept under the table for regular donations. My upbringing and my family history embody generational commitment to giving of oneself and treating others with kindness and respect. Charity, self-sacrifice, and compassion—oftentimes expressed through food and shelter, the most fundamental of our needs— are in my blood.

My family also modeled extending service beyond the essentials and using compassion to empower others. My parents were born in the Dominican Republic and came to the US as adolescents. Not knowing English, my mother struggled to figure out school in the US. In turn, as an adult, she tutored neighborhood children of recently immigrated families with parents who didn't understand English. She brought her "work" home, tutoring these children at our dining room table for years.

To this day, my father is known in our community as a realtor whose kindness extends well past selling houses. Most of his clients moved from New York and didn't have family members nearby to pick their kids up from school when they were sick, nor did they have anyone who could wait around for the plumber. So my father went beyond the duties of even the best realtor, availing himself to these clients and handling these emergencies for them. As was always the way with my parents, he'd be there with an open heart and a willingness to provide support.

My older half-sister became a social worker before I did, and I observed her compassion firsthand when she took me to her volunteer mentoring events and her job at a community center where she developed programming for teens. She taught me the value of discernment and to use that power to help others find solutions to their problems.

MY STRUGGLES

Despite having a loving family, it wasn't picture perfect. Since a near-death experience, my mom has lived with symptoms of PTSD, depression, and agoraphobia. She also became her mother's caretaker after an Alzheimer's diagnosis, fulfilling the Latine tradition of taking care of our elders, regardless of whatever else is going on in our lives. I went from being the center of my mother's world to feeling incredibly alone. My father was always working, and although I had a brother and sister, they were older than me and not around much due to the age gap.

Between my mother's anxiety and grandmother's overprotectiveness, I wasn't allowed to go out or do much. I became quiet, clumsy, and easily distracted. It didn't help that I was overweight, and as much as my mother told me I needed to lose weight, she fed me rice and beans every night. My cousins picked on me, and I had no one to defend me—not even my mother, who lived by the mantra of turning the other cheek. When I told her what was happening or took matters into my own hands by retaliating, she'd remind me, "You never know what's going on in someone else's life that's making them act that way." I felt alone and like my feelings came second to everyone else's. I now understand that aspects of my self-preservation were treated like they didn't matter.

When I was eight, we moved from a cramped Bronx apartment to a house in New Jersey where everyone got their own space. Despite the welcome improvements, I struggled with culture shock. I was one of the only Latine kids in my school. Everyone else was white or Asian, with thin bodies and slick straight hair. I was a chubby Afro Latina with *"pelo malo"* that, despite her best efforts, my mother couldn't tame.

I developed full-blown depression by the time I was nine, but no one knew how to help me. A well-meaning but ultimately misguided guidance counselor asked why I burst into tears randomly in class. She was white, and I doubted that she had ever experienced the sense of alienation I was feeling. I didn't know how to explain to her that I was sad because I hated myself and thought everyone around me did too. Her solution was encouraging me to think of butterflies and to give me ice cream when I got sad. When my parents found me crying, they were unrelenting in asking why I was upset—or screamed at me, letting me know they'd give me a reason to cry if I didn't stop.

I didn't have the words then, so I hid in a dark closet and cried where no one could see me.

College was better, but I still struggled to adjust and keep friends. I had trouble trusting others and went through periods of highs and lows that my peers didn't always understand. At 20, I was diagnosed with bipolar II. I had difficulty concentrating and was diagnosed with ADHD as well. It was hard, and I transferred schools twice before finally graduating.

When I enrolled in a social work graduate program, a friend referred me for a job as a case manager at Adult Protective Services, telling me that her director might let me use the position as a field placement the next semester. Eventually, that director told me another candidate had taken the only fieldwork slot. A different supervisor offered me a placement at the counseling center she ran for survivors of interpersonal violence, but the hours of this placement coincided with my job at Adult Protective Services, and keeping up the lie was hard. I felt anxious and guilty all the time, afraid of getting caught and feeling like I was failing my clients.

This was coupled with difficulties in grad school. I sat at my computer for hours trying to complete papers, frozen and unable to think of anything to write. I failed two classes due to incomplete work. I realized that my bipolar disorder had convinced me to bite off more than I could chew—working full time, going to school full time, and doing my field placement. The anxiety from doing all these things at once was making me depressed and contributed to my difficulty with concentration.

Despite my advisor warning me not to speak to the dean about how my diagnosis affected my ability to complete my work the previous semester, I did it anyway because I assumed that being the dean of a social work school, she'd have some compassion for me. I couldn't have been more wrong. She told me that if I knew I was bipolar, I should have prepared for the semester better. Everything she said after that was a blur. I was finally reaching a breaking point. Between work, school, and general life stress—all exacerbated by my diagnoses, which I was still learning to manage—I was a mess. I'd also had several panic attacks while on public transit that ended with me in the emergency room, and now this.

I walked toward the bus stop in tears, mentally scanning the house for where we kept the pill bottles, thinking that if I took all the pills from all the bottles, there was no way I could survive. I was officially suicidal. But I couldn't do that to my mother. My same mother who had been central to much of my trauma, the one who I blamed for where I was. She was my primary focus at that moment. She'd suffered enough in her life and didn't deserve to lose her child. I had no fight left in me for my own sake, but I could still fight on behalf of my mother. Guilt turned into selflessness turned into self-preservation—a poetic dance that was at once cyclical and, oddly, closure for much of my trauma. I had decided to live for me, for her. It was at this point some really hard work began.

MY HEALING

It took me four years and lots of therapy to work up to re-applying to grad school. Quickly rejected from Rutgers, I was ready to give up, but I'd already started my NYU application, so I sent it and refused to send any others. I prayed to God that if I was truly meant to be a social worker, I'd get in—and I did.

Round two of grad school wasn't easy. I still experienced massive anxiety and panic attacks when a paper was due and rarely handed anything in on time. I should have applied for accommodations, but I never wanted to. I thought I could just push through. It wasn't until my last semester when I started twice-weekly yoga classes at the behest of a friend that I started to feel more at ease, relaxed, and focused. I became mindful of how my body felt and what my body needed. I over-ate less and learned to recognize when my body needs water and other nutrients. I became interested in the mind-body connection and realized how true it is that trauma stays in the body, so healing needs to happen in the body as well.

I'd love to say that my practice became increasingly rigorous, but life is neither simple nor linear. After starting my first post-grad job, I stopped doing yoga for a while. I was depressed and overwhelmed by the stress of the job and how the position pushed against my own values. I slowly found my way back to yoga when I left that job, moving on to work at a community mental health center to provide counseling and coach community-based organization staff on how to teach stress management skills.

In addition to my counseling job, I'm also a part-time therapist at Sandoval CoLab. I got my 200-hour yoga certification, became trained in eye movement desensitization and reprocessing (EMDR) therapy, and was accepted to the Ackerman Institute's Foundations of Family Therapy course. With all these tools, I wish to continue experimenting with healing practices that I can share with the community at large, but especially Black and brown families.

My own healing has taken many forms and has evolved to fit the different circumstances at each stage of my life. For a while, healing took place in a therapist's office (and sometimes still does). It has occurred with friends, family, and mentors who have let me cry on their shoulders and given me validation and words of wisdom. It has also taken place on a yoga mat wet with tears as I released the emotional pain my body holds, and through aromatherapy, learning which scents fit my needs. Most of all, my healing has come through a willingness to experiment, finding out what works for me and accepting how it evolves. Our healing does not need to be linear or prescriptive or exacting. It doesn't always need to involve a specific everyday practice (even though it definitely helps!). There just needs to be a gentle reminder to do the things that help bring you back to center and a process to continue figuring out what those things are.

Ancestral Wisdom:

Tía Fela would say, "Ver por donde no te de la sombra." (Walk in the light.)

Journal Prompts:

1. Reflect on challenging moments during your educational journey. How have you navigated them?
2. What are some tools or practices that you are called to incorporate into your healing journey, and why?
3. Describe resilience. What does it look like for you?

BIOGRAPHY

Michelle Castillo, LCSW works full time as a Program Coordinator at a community-based organization, where she coaches staff on using mental health interventions to support youth in the Coney Island neighborhood and provides psychotherapy to people of all ages, primarily of Latinx backgrounds. She also works part-time as a Psychotherapist at Sandoval CoLab, a group psychotherapy practice, where she provides trauma-informed therapy using mindfulness, somatic therapy, and EMDR. Through her work she strives to provide holistic spaces for others to heal and get the resources they need to lead fulfilling lives.

EYES WIDE OPEN: AWARENESS AS THE KEY TO TRANSFORMATION

REV. DR. JESSICA FLORES, LMSW, MPS

"If we want to see healing and transformation, it's imperative that we don't walk around blinded to root causes."

BLAME AND BELIEF

In my early twenties, I often wondered why I was prone to certain unfavorable thought patterns and behaviors. I wondered the same about people in my community. I had the feeling that my eyes weren't open to the root causes of these issues. As I sought answers to these questions, somehow I knew that this path would lead to healing and transformation. Our thought patterns and behaviors impact our lives, relationships, and social work practice. If we want to see healing and transformation, it's imperative that we don't walk around blinded to root causes.

I was born and raised in the Bronx to a family of Puerto Ricans. I grew up listening to Willie Colon, Biggie Smalls, and Tupac, wearing Reeboks, baggy jeans, and gold door-knocker earrings. My favorite pastime was hanging out on the corner with my friends, talking, laughing, and waiting for my mother to call me in for some rice, beans, and pollo. We would talk about all the hardships we faced in our homes and at school. Our time together, laughing and joking around, was our escape from the harshness and realities of our lives. We shared horrific stories of physical and emotional abuse, but oddly we thought this was the norm. At no point would we have labeled our experiences as domestic violence or systemic injustices—it was just our everyday experience. School didn't teach us about these things either. Our eyes were closed to the reality and causes of our circumstances. We only knew how the experiences made us feel—angry, sad, fearful. We knew something was off, but this was life.

Part of this life was fearing the police because I had witnessed them incarcerate most of my family and friends. Additionally, there was always a story to be told about some form of police brutality against someone in my community. For instance, I had a family member who visited weekly. During their visits, we laughed a lot, and this relative was warm and affectionate. And then there was a month or so they didn't come by. When they eventually returned, they looked the same, but I didn't recognize them. Their spirit was broken. There was no laughter, and there seemed to be a disconnect between us. They had been brutalized by the police, and the resulting trauma left them with long-term mental health challenges. This stirred up something inside of me. Every hardship and injustice I experienced cultivated an intrinsic desire for change and justice for myself, my family, and my community.

In my early years of seeking out how to make change, I had limited knowledge and found myself trying to find someone to blame. Were the police, was it the dominant culture, or was my community to blame when they stepped out of line and somehow broke a law as they were trying to get ahead? This type of inquiry and heartache led me to church. At the time, I didn't know about therapy as a tool for healing. In fact, therapy was stigmatized. So the church was my first point of contact for emotional healing and belonging. As I sat listening to the minister, I heard messages about God's unconditional love and His heart for justice for the marginalized. I held onto scriptures such as Isaiah 30:18-19, "For the Lord is a God of justice. Blessed are all who wait for Him! People of Zion, who live in Jerusalem, you will weep no more." I too wanted justice and to weep no more. As I got closer to God, learning more about Him through meditation on scripture, I was able to reconcile my feelings and what was happening in my community. At church, I learned about forgiveness and understanding that blaming people doesn't bring about change.

The biblical lessons and theology made sense, but I struggled to execute some of the life principles. I didn't realize that my body held unprocessed trauma and moved me toward anxiety, numbness, anger, forgetfulness, and unhealthy coping mechanisms. I saw this struggle reflected in scripture like Romans

7:19-25 NLT, where the disciple Paul wrote, "I want to do what is good, but I don't. I don't want to do what is wrong, but I do it anyway. But if I do what I don't want to do, I am not really the one doing wrong; it is sin living in me that does it."

This cognitive dissonance between the way I wanted to act and how I actually felt wasn't a comfortable place to be. So I had two options: minimize one belief or change the other belief and behavior. At that time, my church community didn't do a great job guiding me in this area. They referred me back to scripture and the idea that there was something wrong with me if I couldn't control my behavior. But I felt deep inside that couldn't be the reason and root cause. This knowledge inspired me to continue to seek healing and a means to bring about transformation for my community. In my journey I found that the key to transformation is self-awareness, awareness of how policy impacts the community, and the incorporation of faith.

TURNING POINTS

Self-awareness and understanding of my drives help me make different decisions. For example, early in my career, I was a social worker providing case management, and my supervisor seemed to be more concerned with numbers than with my well-being or the quality of care our clients were receiving. This was reinforced when my caseload ballooned to over 100, and I started to burn out. It was early on in my inner healing journey, so it was difficult to advocate for myself. However, I mustered up the courage to go to my supervisor for help, but was met with disdain and even more cases added the next day. So I put my head down and got back to work, despite the disappointment and fury building within me. To get through, I learned to practice self-care in my personal time and how to take breaks at work to refresh.

Although my attempt to advocate for myself didn't get me the result I was seeking—a manageable caseload—I found something more valuable. Through processing what was taking place, I discovered that my fear of advocating for myself stemmed from childhood trauma. I had put my supervisor in the place of my primary caregiver and attempted to get acceptance and approval through high performance and voicelessness. This was a pivotal point in my journey. I identified the root cause of my behavior, the feelings I experience when I am placed in similar situations, and the understanding that I can change the narrative. In this case, it meant I could realize that my supervisor wasn't in fact my caregiver, and I'm an adult who has a voice and influence. Through this experience I learned that I wanted to be a different type of leader and that I wanted to have influence over the policies in place to foster healthy environments at work, in relationships, and in my community.

I began to apply this understanding of how to bring healing and transformation on a macro level. I wanted to identify the root causes of the everyday issues my community faced and help change the narrative. I did this by speaking to city officials and influential people in the community to find out the need. Most importantly I went to the source, the community members themselves. I had learned enough to know that addressing issues from my perspective alone would be limiting. I had to extend my reach and get out of my own life experience to learn from others.

In search of root issues for my community's transformation, I discovered a broken system and toxic culture. These perpetuate systemic oppression and the culture of performance and gain as the measure of success, which take a destructive toll on the people under that system and culture. I became inspired to shape my life work around building emotionally healthy leaders, who move from a strengths-based perspective toward policy change and become social justice advocates. Additionally, in my faith community, I've worked to destigmatize mental health challenges and therapy by sharing my experience and equipping faith leaders with the tools to identify when someone is experiencing mental health struggles. The faith leaders now know how to engage, deescalate, and refer someone to professional help. With the aftermath of the pandemic and the current mental health crisis, there's never been a greater need for the church to embrace mental health services.

REFLECTION

Along my journey, I've found that no matter how challenging or dark your experience has been, it can be redeemed. Your past and your behaviors don't define you. The negative experiences in my life moved me to seek out healing and share that with others. The experiences equipped me with the knowledge to speak into another's life who may be navigating what I've been through. There is hope, healing, and transformation when you do the work in therapy and community.

As you move on from this chapter, I urge you to take away the following: Awareness of root issues for both the individual and the community is key for healing and transformation. Looking to the past to process, change the narrative, and move toward healing is only possible when we know where it all stems from. To the next generation of Latinx/e social workers, walk with your eyes wide open. Use what you see to help others heal and thrive.

Ancestral Wisdom:

My titi Sara would say, "Educate yourself, take care of your body, and pass that wisdom on to someone else."

Journal Prompts:

1. Do you understand and know who you are?

2. How comfortable are you in advocating for yourself? What would help you to be more comfortable?

3. What does compassion look like for you, and how do you share it with both yourself and others?

BIOGRAPHY

Rev. Dr. Jessica Flores, LMSW, MPS is a mother, wife, daughter, and aunt. Her passion is to equip families, organizations, and communities to thrive. She is the founder and CEO of Building Leaders Building Community, a business focused on building emotionally healthy leaders through training, executive coaching, life coaching, and consulting. Rev. Dr. Flores also serves as the Executive Director of a family-focused mental health program at a community-based organization in Harlem, working on a grass-roots level towards community transformation. She also serves as an associate pastor and elder at an urban church in the Bronx, New York.

HEALING TO HELP OTHERS HEAL

MADELINE MALDONADO, LCSW-R

"My empathy for other people has grown profoundly from the suffering I have endured throughout my life. I've used my experiences of healing from trauma to help heal others."

LEARNING TO SURVIVE

Walking onto campus 19 years after I graduated, now here to speak to the next generation of social workers, was surreal. I was flooded with memories of my time at New York University. I was also feeling nervous, and I couldn't figure out why. As I looked around the room at all the faces, it dawned on me that I was walking into my destiny as a speaker, teacher, professor, and guide for the social work's next generation. I also recognized how much it meant to the students to see me up there speaking, sharing my experience as a Latinx social worker. It was a deep reminder that representation matters, and I was determined to represent for my people in a way that was never done for me when I was a student.

NYU speaking opportunities weren't something I could have imagined in childhood. I grew up in a part of New York City where violence was common. I can still remember seeing blood in the entryway of my building from someone who had been robbed and stabbed as they were coming home. I don't remember if the man died, but I do remember that we were always hypervigilant in that community. My father carried a legal, licensed handgun, and my mother always had her razor-sharp seamstress scissors tucked into her waistband or bra. My parents weren't violent people, but they immigrated to New York during one of the city's most dangerous eras. It was a tough place to raise a family for anyone, but even more so for Latinx immigrants in a working-poor community affected by lootings during the blackout of 1976 and under siege throughout the crack epidemic of the 1980s. My parents raised me with the clear message that our neighborhood could be very dangerous, and I needed to know how to defend myself.

That lesson began to crystallize when I was bullied in grade school. My intelligence made me the target of negative attention, and even though I never got into a physical fight with my bullies, I learned to fight back with sarcastic insults so that they wouldn't think I was afraid of them—even though I was.

Once high school started, I had to grow up fast. My hour-long commute from the Bronx to Brooklyn Technical

High School meant that I was navigating two worlds. At this specialized high school, I was in classrooms with some of the brightest students in New York. But on the commute to and from school, I was constantly exposed to violence and had to develop street smarts to match my book smarts. Assaults and robberies, gang initiations, men exposing themselves—I saw it all, and more than once. As a girl, I was subjected to a second layer of violence, with men catcalling me, following me down the street, and standing too close to me on the subway. And other girls threatened me and tried to fight me over boys they had crushes on. I was fortunate to be friends with boys who protected me. Some walked me to the subway from school, others took the train to the Bronx with me. Some were even willing to physically fight to protect me from other guys who were harassing me or invading my space. I don't have a living brother, so these friends took on that brotherly role and shielded me as best they could. I developed coping tools to help me survive—mean walking, mean mugging (this generation's "resting bitch face"), verbal aggression, cursing, and being willing to defend myself with violence if needed. Even though this is all a normal part of growing up as a New York Latina, for the sensitive and emotional teenager I was, it was traumatic. It conditioned me to always have my guard up and monitor my environment to ensure safety and survival.

WHEN WILL THE VIOLENCE END?

I thought going to college and living in the dorms would be my escape from violence. But at 19, an ex-boyfriend attacked me while trying to force me to continue our relationship. As the struggle ensued, I thought about Nicole Brown Simpson, who had just died from domestic violence. That thought and my intense fear fueled a strength I didn't know I had in me. That day, I learned that I'll do whatever is necessary to defend my life, and I am proud that I'm still here.

But it didn't end that day. After he was discharged from police custody, he started to stalk me. He waited for me at the subway station by my workplace and called my office so frequently that my job reprimanded me for "distracting" the other employees. I don't remember anyone ever naming what I was experiencing as domestic violence (DV) or intimate partner violence (IPV), or telling me that it was illegal. No one ever pointed me in the direction of help. Not my boss who I confided in about the stalking. Not my college professor who read the nine-page essay I wrote about the experience and trauma—I just received an A- and a few corrections on my sentence structure and grammar.

It wasn't just that ex either. As a 22-year-old social work student, I dated someone who was prone to drastic mood swings and angry outbursts. When I finally had enough, I told him it was over, but he got it into his head that I was leaving him for someone else. He flew into a rage, attacking me and destroying my apartment. But again, no one ever named this as DV, IPV, assault, or abuse, not even his mother when I told her about his outbursts and bad temper. He was far from the last of my partners to verbally abuse me, cross my boundaries, and traumatize me.

I know that I am very lucky to have survived two attacks, both without permanent physical injuries. More than a quarter of women under 50 have experienced IPV at least once, according to the World Health Organization. And according to the CDC, homicide is the fourth leading cause of death for girls under 20, and the fifth leading cause of death for women aged 20-44. Gendered violence is so bad that in 2021, the United States declared a femicide epidemic—an epidemic of women killed by men in intimate settings. IPV claims the lives of three women every day.

Violence wormed its way into my professional life too. In September 2001, I was a frontline worker providing therapy to clients who survived 9/11, and two months later, countless clients of mine lost family members when American Airlines Flight 587 crashed on its way from New York to the Dominican Republic. I had the dual experience of supporting my traumatized clients while reeling from nightmares and debilitating flight anxiety myself. A year later, I got into a car accident with coworkers who were also my close friends, but the aftermath of blame, rumors, and officewide division led to ending those friendships, mistrusting colleagues wherever I worked, and building internal walls to keep from experiencing that kind of hurt again. Every time a boss targeted me with microaggressions or whenever an employee I supervised punctured my tires, ripped up work in my face, or cursed me out, those walls felt justified.

Not even home was safe either. Once, my next-door neighbor attempted to assault me as I was leaving for work.

When I moved to a new apartment, a contractor I hired became obsessed with us having a romantic relationship, harassing me with calls and texts. I had to get the police involved and pay a locksmith $300 to change all the locks so that I was protected from the contractor.

LEARNING TO HEAL

Experiencing such a range and frequency of violence distorted my life. I coped in ways that were destructive, and my body learned to be on high alert. My fight or flight instinct simmered just below the surface, ready to kick in at a moment's notice—and it did. The trauma and resulting triggers made me emotionally detached and dysregulated, leaving me to act in ways that weren't aligned with my values. Someone in Hollywood once said, "Love will make you do crazy things." My take on that is, "Trauma will make you do crazy things."

It's critical for social workers to know that clients aren't the only ones with trauma. Our trauma—the trauma that predates or is independent of our careers, the trauma we experience because of the systemic violence in the profession, all of it—influences how we show up in our work. It can manifest as perfectionism, excessive worrying, overworking, and anger.

I've seen many social workers self-sabotage, dull their own brilliance, and lose their ability to contribute to others' healing because they weren't willing to do their own work to heal. I've seen colleagues lose their jobs and careers because of drinking at work, time theft, falsifying medical records and billing, inappropriate behavior toward clients, and insubordination. I've also seen many competent social workers struggling with uncontrollable anxiety, substance use, alcohol dependence, depression, and PTSD. When you don't work on your healing, burnout is inevitable.

I've chosen to heal, and I will continue to choose healing even when it's so difficult that I have screamed for minutes in my car from the pain and anguish. I will choose healing even when it means ugly crying myself to sleep and waking up with puffy eyes and a wad of tissues in my fist. I've had to forgive over and over and show people grace who haven't deserved it. I have apologized to people I've harmed with my words and actions—having experienced trauma does not excuse you from taking accountability for yourself. I've had to let go of people, places, jobs, and things that don't serve my mental health, my healing, and my growth as a human. I've had to educate myself about the warning signs of abusive and toxic friendships and romantic relationships. I had to learn to not ignore red flags or downplay them because I can see the good in everyone and in every situation. I've learned to remain calm in the face of someone's rage and threats of violence so that I can properly assess my response, de-escalate them, and take appropriate action. I've had to learn to assert myself, my rights, and my boundaries within personal and professional relationships. I've also sought help via healthy channels such as psychotherapy, acupuncture, reiki, meditation, and going to church. This is in addition to exercising, daily prayer, journaling, and going on vacation four times a year to disconnect from the world and connect with myself.

My empathy for other people has grown profoundly from the suffering I have endured throughout my life. I've used my experiences of healing from trauma to help heal others. I've chosen to release the painful experiences I've had and see them as lessons that have helped me develop into an incredibly empathic and resilient person. Today I am a peaceful, happy woman who can resolve conflicts and help people heal in ways that still amaze me!

So when I stepped in front of the classroom of emerging NYU social workers, I brought every part of myself—the daughter of Latinx immigrants, the survivor of violence, the traumatized New Yorker, the healing work in progress, and the healing partner to clients and my community. I was there to show them how all my experiences, good and bad, made me the social worker I am today. I was there to remind the next generation of social workers to embrace their imperfections, their journeys, and their desire to heal themselves and the world.

Ancestral Wisdom:

My mother taught me to seek God, trust Him, and rely on my faith during hard times. She also taught me to have courage and pick myself up after failures and disappointments: "Cuando caes, tienes que levantarte. Mañana es un nuevo día."

Journal Prompts:
1. Name some instances in your life that you have experienced violence. How have you dealt with them?
2. How have these experiences of violence shown up in your behaviors and relationships?

3. What steps can you take to initiate healing?

BIOGRAPHY

Madeline Maldonado, LCSW-R has over 20 years of experience in program administration, clinical supervision, psychotherapy, diagnostic evaluations, and social work consulting. Madeline's greatest joy is to motivate and inspire her clients and other professionals as an agent of hope and change.

Madeline is the president & founder of Madeline Maldonado, LCSW Consulting P.C. providing social work consulting services for children referred by the NYC Early Intervention Program. She is the co-founder and President of Minette LCSW Psychotherapy Services PLLC, a clinic that specializes in culturally humble psychotherapy for Latino and BIPOC children, adults, and families. Madeline is also an adjunct professor at Fordham University's MSW Program.

She received a Master's Degree from New York University Silver School of Social Work.

www.minettepsychotherapy.com

madeline.maldonadolcswr@gmail.com

Instagram: @minettepsychotherapy

LinkedIn: www.linkedin.com/in/mmaldonado-lcswr/

Linktree: linktr.ee/MadelineMaldonado

KELLY PACHECO, LMSW

"I may have questioned many things, but the passion and drive I learned from my Head Start families never wavered."

HAPPINESS AND HELPLESSNESS

In my cubicle sat a young mother of three sobbing, thanking me for choosing her child to receive the Thanksgiving basket created from all the donated goods from the Head Start's food drive. Having worked with this family for two school years, I was aware of their financial and emotional struggles at home. I knew they needed the basket more than many others, but I wasn't prepared to realize just how much.

"Yo me preguntaba cómo iba a darles de comer a los niños

hoy, no tengo ni una gota de aceite en la casa," ("I asked myself how I was going to feed the kids today, I don't even have a drop of oil at home") the young mom said as she quietly cried.

I was overwhelmed by emotion. I was happy to be able to provide some relief, but I knew it was nowhere near enough. Nothing I could do would be enough. That sliver of happiness was overshadowed by helplessness and even shame. I thought of all the moments I had wasted food myself and how many times this family must've gone to bed hungry. I asked myself how many more families found themselves in the same circumstances and don't have the support they need.

HER, MY JOURNEY

I began my journey into social work when my own young mother was pursuing her social work degree. As an immigrant, she has always struggled with grammar and writing, so at 13, I spent a lot of time proofreading her college-level assignments. I was always so proud to be helpful and was eager to learn more about the topics she discussed in her writing. Social work became something that connected us because it was uniquely ours.

As she worked her way through school, I saw how my mom struggled to juggle her scarce time between two jobs, classes, internship, and parenting. At times, I hated social work because it was the thing that took her away from our family. But its importance held strong as I grew older. My teen and young adult years were spent fighting the obvious path of following in my mother's footsteps. I constantly questioned if this was something

I wanted to do simply because it's what I knew or if it was actually within me to do it. I questioned so much and traveled different paths before arriving right back where it had all started.

After high school, I planned to be an FBI special agent, so I enrolled in John Jay College. I was determined to do something other than what my mom did, so I combined my passion for psychology with my love for crime shows. But the deeper I got into the criminology curriculum, the more I knew it wasn't going to make me happy. My criminology major eventually switched to forensic psychology with a minor in sociology. As I continued to explore what I was drawn to, I kept fighting the urge to run down the social work path. But that path began to chase me when I landed the position of family worker at a Head Start program.

Being a family worker had been vaguely described to me when I was looking for a job that would be more career-oriented, aka a "big girl" job. I wasn't entirely sure of the job description when I walked into the interview, and I remember sitting with other candidates who looked 10 times more sure of themselves. When I got the position, after three rounds of interviews with directors and parents, I was still very skeptical of how much I was prepared to be in this role. I quickly—and I mean quickly—felt the pressure of how much I still had to learn when I was sent on a home visit a week into starting. What was a home visit? I had no idea. But I was lucky enough to have a helpful teacher with me, who took her time to guide me as much as she could.

FIREFIGHTING

As I navigated my new role, it became apparent how much was expected of me yet how limited the resources available were. I was catapulted into what felt like a mine field because the moment I thought I had one thing figured out, something else exploded. I wanted so badly to do well because I had my own history in this place—it was the same Head Start program I attended as a toddler—and it felt almost like karmic intervention that I had ended up there. But my journey was full of challenges. Every day felt like I was running from one fire to another, putting one out just to find out another had started. While I experienced many rewarding moments, there were far more concerns than I would've thought possible.

Working in a community that I grew up in, in a community that raised me and was part of my core, gave me the drive I needed to succeed. I was lucky enough to also have a strong familial support system to go with it. My own story often lingered in my head. I was the American-born child to teen immigrant parents, parents who had the odds stacked against them. Yet I grew up always feeling supported and sheltered from the times we struggled. It wasn't perfect; my parents divorced, I rebelled, we faced many challenges rooted in their trauma and my own struggle to make sense of cultural differences. But I always knew I was blessed to have the support my family gave me.

So much of my upbringing was mirrored back to me when I worked with the Head Start families. There were simply never enough resources to go around, and I was plagued with guilt about my own circumstances and anger at the things that were out of my control. I questioned, what was the difference between these families and my own? What could I do to help them get what they needed to succeed? My list of questions could go on and on, but one thing I didn't question anymore was that I needed to be a social worker.

The reality is that I have yet to answer many of those questions because I continue to walk down my unique path as a social worker. What I do know is that the families I encountered in my days as a family worker sealed my decision to reach the same destination my mom always talked about. As I finished my undergrad degree, moved onto graduate studies, began my internship, and started my career, I questioned many things, but the passion and drive I learned from my Head Start families never wavered. As I continue to work toward a variety of professional goals, the constant that remains is doing what I can to make a difference, no matter how small, in the lives of those who need it most.

From growing up together in life to growing up together as professionals, with continued growth to come: thank you for always guiding me, my madrina and mom Mariana Lopez.

Ancestral Wisdom:

I am you, you are me, we are one.

Journal Prompts:

1. What fuels you? How can you do a little bit of what you are passionate about every day?

2. In the same way we take care of others, we must also take care of ourselves. What are you doing to care for yourself?

BIOGRAPHY

Kelly Pacheco, LMSW is currently the Chief Operating Officer at Lifeskills Counseling Services, as well as the MSW Research Assistant at Weill Cornell Medicine. She began her career in family social work at a Head Start program.

Kelly holds a BA in Forensic Psychology from John Jay University and a Master of Social Work from New York University.

BRIDGING CULTURES AND HEALING
PATHS: A JOURNEY IN PSYCHEDELIC
THERAPY AND SOCIAL WORK

CAMILA PASTOR, LCSW, SEP

"So, here you are
too foreign for home
too foreign for here.
Never enough for both."
—*Ijeoma Umebinyuo, Diaspora Blues*

THREE CULTURES, ONE CHILDHOOD

I am a Latina clinical social worker and third-culture kid (TCK) originally from Peru. TCK refers to individuals who have spent a significant part of their developmental years in a culture outside their parents' culture(s) due to accompanying caretakers abroad for work or due to other factors such as immigration. The concept of the "third culture" encapsulates the unique blend that emerges within TCKs, combining elements of their native culture (the first culture) with that of their current residence (the second culture), resulting in a distinct and multifaceted third cultural identity. Often, TCKs develop connections to multiple cultures without fully belonging to anyone.

In my case, I was born in New York City, my mother is Chilean, and my father Peruvian. We relocated to Spain, Chile, and eventually Peru at age 12. As a result, I learned to navigate a blend of American cultural influences from my upbringing in New York and Peruvian cultural experiences from my time living in Peru. This interplay shaped my identity, worldview, and cultural affiliations, contributing to the formation of a third culture that has integrated aspects of both cultures. When people ask me where I am from, I wonder if they're asking about where I live now, where I grew up, or my ethnicity. As a third-culture kid I mainly identify as Peruvian, so I usually say, "I am Peruvian, but grew up in New York and Peru." Being a TCK, I internalized the belief that there's never *one* right way to do something. I grew up in a constant state of genuine curiosity, loosely holding what I defined as "normal" and appreciating the richness of existing at diverse crosspoints.

When my family and I first moved to Peru in the early 1980s, I was not happy about the move at all. I was going into puberty and leaving behind very exciting things in the United States like the new MTV network, big hair, and bright colors, for a poor developing country with complex social inequities. I was resentful and didn't understand my parents' choice to live in such a perplexing country. After the initial bumpy adjustment, I settled in, made friends, learned to read and write proficiently, and found my place. That said, I still struggled with a lot of social nuance and eventually found my way back to New York as a college transfer student. I studied architecture and design and lived in that world for a decade.

Once I had children I started thinking more about my culture of origin, my Hispanic heritage, and how it fit into my life. I seemed to have lost some of it along the way, especially as a TCK, and I wrestled with determining what parts felt true to me. I had no family in the US and the yearly trips to Peru kept my life siloed in some ways, never really integrating my two worlds. I started to look for a new challenge, feeling called to make a difference in a meaningful way. Social justice has always been a recurring theme in my life, coming from a poor country and seeing so many immigrants in New York City facing difficulties that I had the privilege to skirt due to my American passport. I was inspired to take action and was accepted to New York University's Master in Social Work program. The program opened my eyes to many systemic problems the Latinx communities face and opened my heart to have faith that change can happen—social work can make a difference in people's lives.

As part of my MSW training I took an internship at a community center servicing the Latinx population. This internship started my journey to slowly reconnecting back to and loving my culture—the richness of the community, its nuance and individuality. I am forever grateful for the experience and ended up working at the community center for years. I worked mostly in Spanish with clients that felt both seen and safe in a place where they could be understood. I learned about Dominican, Colombian, Ecuadorian, Venezuela, Mexican culture—any and all Latin American countries. I also learned more of their struggles and the difficulties of migrating for their American Dream.

TRANSFORMATIVE HEALING:
MIND, BODY, AND SPIRIT

During the years spent at the community center I started to develop my interests in holistic, bottom-up approaches to psychotherapy. I noticed how most of my clients were disconnected from their bodies, jumpy, or disassociated. As my interest grew, I focused on developing my skills in trauma therapy, which led me to study modalities like Somatic Experiencing, Compassionate Inquiry, EMDR, and Internal Family Systems while deepening my knowledge and practice in contemplative traditions. I aimed to foster a deeper mind-body connection for my clients, advocating for alternative tools amidst my concerns of over-medication with psychotropic medications. I felt my clients could benefit from understanding their bodies that carried so much of their lived experience, and empower them to have a better relationship with their bodies to heal deep-seated pain. Although I know there is a place for medication, I believe people need proper informed consent as to how these medicines affect their bodies. I also believe people need to be offered choices in selecting what best fits them. I decided I needed more flexibility to utilize these new approaches. I left public health and started my private practice.

In my quest for diverse therapeutic approaches and going back to my roots, I discovered the transformative potential of psychedelics. This journey brought me back home to Peru and the Shipibo people in the Peruvian Amazon, where I experienced profound healing and teachings that redirected my career path. While Indigenous communities have used psychedelics in therapeutic and religious settings for centuries, psychedelic therapy is relatively new in Western clinical settings, particularly for communities of color. I spent extensive time with the Shipibo, shadowing, assisting, and eventually facilitating healing ceremonies, deepening my understanding of plant medicines and skilled facilitation. Back in New York I enrolled in the MAPS MDMA-assisted psychotherapy training, which not only allowed me to further my growth as a therapist with Non-Ordinary States of Consciousness as a treatment for clients, but also challenged me to look inside and work on my own healing.

In my enthusiasm for psychedelic healing, it dawned on me that a considerable number of my clients ironically would never be able to receive these medicines due to many systemic barriers such as economic and treatment access, stigma related to mental disorders, and lack of access to legal support. My commitment to integrating psychedelics into therapy led me to explore other methods like ketamine assisted psychotherapy, breathwork, and art therapy in my private practice to support clients on their healing journeys in more accessible ways.

I have seen the limitations of traditional top-down talk therapy as I have opened my horizon to new ways of being and knowing, embracing the idea that we all have our inner healing intelligence that, when supported correctly, can take us where we need to go. I am passionate about increasing accessibility and inclusion to psychedelic therapy, particularly within communities that have been underrepresented in this field. For our Latinx community, racial trauma is an overwhelming psychological harm for which we need improved tools to integrate in the therapeutic process. To do so without risking more harm, we need providers that are part of the community.

REFLECTION

Reflecting on my career as a social worker, I am reminded that our society is constantly evolving, and it is our collective responsibility to persist in confronting the challenges that hinder our community's well-being. In our journey, it is crucial to uphold values such as empathy, dedication, fairness, and inclusivity as fundamental pillars of our language and mission.

I have come to understand that self-care is not a mere selfish indulgence as I once thought; it is an *essential* practice that enables us to better support others in need and safeguard our own well-being. Recurring doubts linger within me—have I truly exerted all efforts to make a difference, influence perspectives, and push for positive change? In these moments, I remind myself to uphold self-care. I invite you to ask and journal to yourself:

1. How am I taking care of my physical body, my mind, and my spirit?
2. How am I creating time to laugh, be in nature, eat well, get enough sleep, and exercise?

Ancestral Wisdom:

At the end of the day, money comes and goes, people come and go, and all you really have left is who is looking back at you in the mirror…

BIOGRAPHY

Camila Pastor, LCSW, SEP is a bilingual Licensed Clinical Social Worker and Somatic Experiencing Practitioner working in private practice. Camila currently works as a Ketamine Assisted Psychotherapy (KAP) therapist running individual and BIPOC KAP groups. In Peru, her country of origin, Camila facilitates ayahuasca plant medicine-based journeys, which have been scientifically proven to aid in the healing of depression, anxiety, and substance abuse disorders. Camila volunteers as a child advocate to support undocumented detained minors as they navigate the criminal justice system. She has been a Big Sister since 1999 at Bigs & Littles NYC Mentoring, where she has served on the board. Camila is currently a board member at Inanna Rising, a collective of psychedelic medicine and therapeutic clinicians, on their Indigenous and Racial Equity and Access Honoring Committee.

Camila Pastor LCSW Psychotherapy
camilapastor.com
IG: camilapastorlcsw
LinkedIn: camila-pastor-lcsw-sep

BYANKA RAMOS, LCSW

"I knew I wanted to help children. I knew I wanted to work with communities that looked like the ones I grew up in. I just didn't know how I could do that. Until I found social work."

SEEDS OF SHAME

Shame is an emotion that anchors us down, limits our growth, and isolates us. Shame is powerful—it unknowingly controlled much of my life. It wasn't until I found mentors in the field of social work who helped me untangle the roots of my shame that I could move forward freely. Social work is not only transformational to those we serve, but to every social worker who practices the profession. Finding social work was a catalyst for overcoming the shame I carried with me.

I was born and raised in Houston, Texas, a city known for its diversity at the intersection of so many nationalities and ethnicities. My family proudly showcased their Mexican and Chicano roots. My father loved low-riders, Dickies, Pachuco hats, and Locs sunglasses. We went to flea markets and looked for Homies dolls to collect. There was no lack of Brown Pride in my childhood—my father even has this tattooed on his forearms. Despite the pride that radiated throughout my family, all I felt was shame.

I was born to teen parents who lacked the skills and resources to properly care for me. My mother, who was also raising my older brother, didn't have much support. When she made the decision to leave my father, my paternal grandmother, my Wuela, worried for my safety and asked her to leave me in her care.

Living with my Wuela meant I lived in a home full of tíos, tías, y primos. Under her care, we were never without food, clean clothes, and love. It seems like this would be a joyous way to live, but as we know, life is complicated. In reality, our home was full of domestic violence, struggles with substances and alcohol, and money problems. With so much conflict and never having a room of my own, I escaped into television and books. In the '90s, television families looked nothing like mine. In those shows, families lived in two-story homes, not apartments. Children slept in their own beds, in their own rooms. There wasn't yelling and hitting. In those shows, all those people were white. So in my head, it was clear: Being brown came with trauma, and being white came with success. I had to find a way to get into white spaces.

The only way I could do this was through education. School was my haven. I excelled in elementary school and loved the attention I got from doing so well. There, it didn't matter where I lived and who was raising me. I wasn't the girl whose parents were gone. At school, I wasn't judged by things I had no control over. I was important, and people noticed. My Wuela and the rest of my family always bragged about how smart I was. They would brag that I was going to be the first to graduate high school and go to college. I thrived under the pressure, and I was sure that if I just kept pushing, I would achieve success and have a life I could be proud of.

My elementary school principal also noticed. She often praised my intelligence and character, and when she took a job at a private school, she recruited me. My Tía, who had become another maternal figure to me, was extremely excited for this opportunity. She told me it was clear that going to this private school was the pathway to achieving all my goals. The admission process tested me rigorously—interviews, shadowing, and exams—each step creating new insecurities. Despite initial doubts, I was accepted, unaware then of the profound impact this change would have on my future.

ENTERING A WHITE SPACE

Going to a public school, I wasn't aware that the financial struggles my family experienced were remarkable. I was a student who didn't lack clothes, nice shoes, or food. My dad, although not present to offer parental guidance, always made sure to provide financial support. In public school, I was one of the "well-off students." But before even stepping foot onto my new private school campus, I became hyper-aware that my family was struggling. When the school referred us to their uniform vendor, everything I needed was way out of our budget. We ended up buying the dress shirts, blazers, and dress shoes second-hand, and one of my relatives made the gray skirts I needed. It was a different fabric than everyone else's, and when I was asked where I got my skirts, I was so embarrassed.

Stepping onto the campus was like entering a new world. As I walked the halls, I noticed that most students didn't look like me. Their skin was pale and freckled, and they had blonde, straight, thin hair. My hair was thick, dark, and wavy. Even though I'm considered *guera,* my skin was olive in comparison. They had perfect white teeth or braces to help them get there. My smile was crooked. My appearance made me stand out immediately. Still, I had hope that my intelligence would allow me to blend in, that I would excel academically and be accepted.

But the academic rigor of this school was lightyears ahead of my public school. Every class had textbooks, like in college. Every teacher spoke with a vocabulary that I couldn't understand. I would be up until midnight finishing homework. I started failing assignments and eventually failing classes. The shame hit. This time it felt different, though. School was the place where I belonged, where so much of my self-worth came from, and now, that was gone. I was so confused and ashamed. I wasn't as smart as I thought I was. I wasn't as special as I thought I was. My whole identity was shattered in a matter of months.

I didn't want to tell my family what was going on. They had been bragging to neighbors, family members, and acquaintances about the nice school I was going to and how smart I was. I couldn't bring myself to disappoint them and tell them that I hated the school. I had to find a way to figure this out. Eventually, I got myself to pass my classes, and the next year was better, at least academically. I told myself, it's okay that you're not smart, it's okay that you're just average, people like you aren't meant to be special.

I managed to find some people who looked like me at school. A Mexican, brown-skinned, Spanish-speaking girl enrolled when I was in high school. During one conversation about our identities, she said she identified as Mexican because she was born in Mexico, and when I told her that my family had always told me I was Chicana, her face scrunched up in disgust. "Ew, I would never call myself that. My mom said Chicanos are dirty and working class." Immediate shame hit. This was the first time that I realized that not every Mexican or brown person grew up like me. I wasn't different just because I was Chicana; it was because I was poor, too. My classmate may have shared my culture, but her classism proved she did not share my experiences.

From then on, I called myself Hispanic because it sounded more acceptable and palatable.

Despite the difficulties, I managed to graduate, get into college, and get scholarships. To my family, the mission was accomplished. And without a self-identity, with lots of shame, and with no expectation of success, I went off to college.

FINDING SOCIAL WORK, GROWING OUT OF SHAME

As you can imagine, entering college with those feelings didn't lead to success. After my first year, I dropped out. I had no sense of purpose or direction and no guidance from anyone I trusted. I had learned that no one would understand where I was coming from or how to help me. For years after high school, I worked full time, but my heart always called me back to school. I re-enrolled in community colleges but would stop attending after a while. It wasn't until I became pregnant that this changed. The weight of carrying life inside me made me determined to figure out who I was and who I wanted to be. I knew I wanted my child to have parents with college degrees, who could help her navigate education, who could help her achieve her goals. I thought having a degree would make me a better mother.

I sat down and looked through every single major listed on the nearest community college's website. I knew I wanted to help children. I knew I wanted to work with communities that looked like the ones I grew up in. I just didn't know how I could do that. Until I found social work. Up until that point, I only knew of case workers who worked in social service agencies. Once I read the description, I realized how much more social workers could do, and I felt like it would be a good fit. I chose that as my major, but was still plagued by negative self-talk. I told myself, you just have to finish this degree; you have already taken long enough.

It wasn't until I finished with online community college and stepped onto a four-year university campus again that transformation happened. I went to my first in-person social work class, and I was moved. My professor was short and Chicana, like me. She had long gray hair, and she spoke fiercely and unapologetically. Throughout the semester, she challenged all of us to rethink how we saw the world around us and how we saw ourselves. She talked about her challenges, she was passionate about her causes, and she made me feel seen. Professor Medina was one of my first mentors, and she didn't even know it. All she had to do was stand in front of the classroom and represent herself. As I watched her teach, I began to love school, seeing how I could be brown and still succeed. For the first time in my life, I saw another Chicana I wanted to be like.

I wanted to do more than get by. I wanted to be the best social worker I could be. I assumed I would get there by getting good grades and writing the best papers. When I scored low on an assignment, I stayed after to talk with her, disappointed in myself. She looked at me and said, "You really are overthinking this. Your grade does not make you a better or worse person." For all my life, I had tied my worth to my academic achievements, and with one sentence my professor released me from this expectation.

After meeting her, I met other badass Latina professors in social work and other amazing social work mentors. I felt a freedom to be myself, to explore my interests without tying them to achievements, and I felt pride in my culture. This is what allowed me to excel. I realized that my family is not something to be ashamed of, and in fact, I should be proud of their accomplishments and resilience. Through the trauma of their own lives, they made sure I had basic necessities, made sure I was loved, and provided me with support, even when I felt I wasn't worthy of it. For so long I tried to not be like them, but after so much reflection and life experience, I hope to be as resilient as them, as strong as them, and as proud as them to be Chicana.

I carry all these lessons with me now as a school social worker. I work with students whose stories are like mine, and it is amazing to see a reflection of my younger self in them. My hope is to make them feel seen, valued, and part of a community that welcomes, accepts, and celebrates them for all of who they are. I want them to know that their worth and value aren't tied to grades, who their parents are, where they live, or any other arbitrary societal marker of success. I want this for my students, for my children, and for every single person who feels shame about who they are. I don't want it to take 26 years for them to know they are worthy just because they exist.

A special thank you to my Madrina in this book, Evelyn Bautista-Miller, for her support and guidance.

Ancestral Wisdom:

My wuela and tía taught me that pride comes not from awards or arbitrary accomplishments, but from the way we take care of others and the way we navigate the world around us.

Journal Prompts

1. What parts of you do you hide and feel ashamed of?
2. Who has helped you in your journey, and can you take a piece of that mentorship to support your self-worth?
3. What defines your worth and what are your indicators of success?

BIOGRAPHY

Byanka Ramos, LCSW, is a dedicated school social worker based in San Antonio, Texas. She graduated with a Bachelor's in Social Work from Our Lady of the Lake University, the oldest social work school in Texas, in 2018. She then earned her Master's in Social Work from the University of Texas at San Antonio in 2019.

Byanka has a diverse background in social work, with experience in aiding unhoused individuals, LGBTQ+ communities, and victims of violence and trauma. However, her true passion lies in working youth labeled at-risk. She has been a school social worker for four years, specializing in serving students in alternative education settings, those with behavioral issues, and supporting campus Social and Emotional Learning (SEL) initiatives.

In addition to her role in schools, Byanka also works as a therapist at a behavioral health hospital. She has organized and chaired the Oiga Mi Voz LaTeena Youth Conference, which promotes positive cultural identity among young Latinas. Byanka is passionate about Latina causes, proud to be Chicana, and committed to spreading cultural pride.

Byanka lives in San Antonio with her husband and two children.

ARLYS TINEO, LMSW

"If you talk to a man in a language he understands, that goes to his head. If you talk to him in his language, that goes to his heart." —Nelson Mandela

NI DE AQUÍ NI DE ALLÁ

When I was four, my parents decided to move out of the only Latino neighborhood in the county. They achieved the American dream of owning a home to raise their two young daughters. We moved from our small two-bedroom apartment to a two-story house in a White suburban neighborhood just 30 minutes north of New York City.

One of my earliest memories is sitting in the living room with Mami doing my reading and writing homework after a busy day as a first grader. I dreaded doing homework because it meant sitting in the living room for hours while Mami skimmed through an English-Spanish dictionary trying to help me. I could see the frustration in Mami's face as she struggled to understand the homework instructions. By nine years old, I was translating legal immigration forms and scheduling doctor's appointments for my parents. On more than one occasion, I was picked up early from school because my parents needed an interpreter during appointments. At eleven years old, I started working with Papi at his bodega, selling lotto scratch-offs and listening to the town's chisme.

Throughout grade school, I felt displaced, unwelcomed, and singled out by my peers. It wasn't until I got older that I realized how naïve I had been for not seeing these microaggressions for what they were. During the day, I was speaking English and listening to my classmates talk about an upcoming slumber party or the luxurious vacations they went on. But at school, I was known as the girl who was "too Hispanic" because I ate beans for lunch or spoke Spanish on occasion. It didn't help that I was placed in a speech program in elementary school because of my accent. At night, I was speaking Spanish and pleading with Mami for permission to let me hang out with my friends for a couple of hours. Mami would say, "Tú crees que eres americana" (You think you are an American). It's the living definition of the famous Latino phrase: "Ni de aquí ni de allá" (from neither here nor there). I would explain to my parents every day that growing up in the campos of Bonao and the busy barrios of Santo Domingo are very different from the small, quiet, American town they were raising their daughters in. During my early teenage years, my mental health started to suffer. I developed depression and anxiety from the cultural differences and the inability to truly express myself in various environments. As a teenager, I didn't know any better and felt alone in this overwhelming experience.

My relationship with religion has always been complex. But I was taught I could pray whenever and wherever I wanted. On days when I felt the most alone and out of place, I would pray in my head, "Please make me normal." I attended church (almost) every Sunday and when asked to pray after receiving the Eucharist, I'd kneel on the church pew and question God for giving me this life. My teenage mind strongly believed that praying to a higher power was the solution to my identity crisis of leading a double life.

THE SEARCH FOR LANGUAGE ACCESS

It wasn't until the age of 18, when I moved out of my small tight-knit community to the diverse city of Brooklyn, that I surrounded myself with minorities from all corners of the world. It was an eye-opening experience for a young Latina discovering herself. I developed relationships with other young Latinos and individuals of color. I quickly realized the universality of our experiences and felt comforted by our shared backgrounds and values. Self-acceptance was the first true step in my healing journey. It was then that I developed the language for what being a first-generation American truly meant.

Self-reflection became paramount for me during this time. I felt ashamed of the resentment I held for my parents, for moving our family to a new neighborhood and giving me immense responsibility at an early age. Through therapy and my social work journey, I've accepted that my parents did what they thought was best for their two American-born daughters.

I started identifying which factors or social determinants would have improved our "American Dream" and relieved the burden of a first-generation family. I realized that many of my parent's struggles, then inherited to me, were caused mainly by lack of language access.

This revelation allowed me to identify a passion for language access—a basic human right for non-English speakers. I became frustrated when learning that the Civil Rights Act, Executive Orders, and numerous laws are in place to ensure language accessibility, yet are not enforced by the government. If my parents had been provided access to Spanish interpreters, maybe they wouldn't have relied on me to make phone calls. Maybe my parents wouldn't have pulled me out of school early to translate a doctor's appointment. Maybe they wouldn't have needed me to read every letter that arrived in the mail. Maybe they wouldn't have transferred their anxiety of entering English-dominated spaces onto me.

Social work further opened my eyes to the injustices stemming from lack of language access as I witnessed my clients deterred from seeking help due to the lack of services in Spanish. For instance, while working in psychiatry, I met an elderly woman who described feeling immense relief when I spoke Spanish to her. I remember countless other examples: meeting clients who wish to enroll in courses to increase their income and inspire their children but are discouraged by the lack of Spanish-led trade schools. Meeting individuals who are unable to advocate for themselves due to the lack of translators and interpreters. Meeting parents who feel helpless when their children have questions with homework. Meeting clients receiving documentation and forms in English who feel frustrated when they are unable to understand them. To make matters worse, parents then rely on their children as interpreters; not because they want to, but as a means of survival. The injustices surrounding language access angered the little girl inside me who would have benefitted from interpretation services for my parents.

As a social worker, I'm always hearing about the latest community, state, health, or other social program. After realizing the lack of language access in these initiatives, I started to question whether most programs were accessible and beneficial to non-English speakers. Language continues to be pertinent regarding documentation, client communication, outreach, and policy. Lack of language access has trickled down to community agencies, government, and healthcare resulting in a domino effect in the quality of service provision.

The use of translation lines and interpretation services is crucial, alongside the communication for staff to know the services are available. Nowadays, many systems allow for scheduling interpreters in advance to reduce delays. An initiative started in rural hospitals in Kansas and Missouri proved that the simple increase of telephones for staff increased the usage of interpretation lines in all areas of the hospitals. It makes a big difference in service provision—not only will the client be comfortable, but it will begin a trusting relationship with them. The coronavirus pandemic increased the use of technology in all aspects of life, allowing for remote interpreting technology to take the place of in-person interpreters. Such a system allows interpreters from other locations to increase interpretation access.

The reliance on bilingual family members often replaces trained professionals, although it's documented that untrained translators misinterpret or omit important phrases which may have important consequences. As the risk of dangerous errors in communication increases, so do the emotional difficulties for the family members. The emotional toll is especially present for children as the pressure to translate is part of their day-to-day lives. Children are too often burdened with translating for their loved ones for a multitude of reasons—out of respect, responsibility, and the demands of parents. Children are quick to oblige due to their instincts to take on the role of translator. However, the burden of that responsibility goes unnoticed in the moment. The emotional toll I experienced while translating for my parents still weighs on me. I often feel angry thinking about how hard I was on myself for not being able to do a good job with difficult translations, like medical terms, when that never should have been my responsibility in the first place.

The burden carries over to bilingual clinicians and social workers as well. Being the only bilingual employee at work became common, and I quickly realized I was experiencing the same translation burdens with clients as with my parents. Bilingual social workers often replace the use of interpreter lines for faster interpreting; however, this comes at the cost of higher burnout rates, the inability to effectively manage work responsibilities, and the retraumatization or trigger to an inner childhood wound. This highlights the difference between bilingual and monolingual workers in the field. Social work agencies must start investing in training employees as professional interpreters or increase salaries for employees to perform the additional responsibility of interpreting with clients.

Even now as an adult, it's common for my family to ask for translation help, whether it be mail, a flyer, or other documents. If paperwork was provided in Spanish, my parents could focus on appointments without having to depend on me to translate their documents beforehand. This has trickled down into my professional life, as clients often send me screenshots of emails and documents in Spanish.

I've realized that reading documentation in English is a privilege. Consent forms in multiple languages are crucial for clients to comprehend what they're signing and for future reference; not to mention also embedded in the social work code of ethics. For bilingual social workers, we often play the role of translator and read entire forms to a client, resulting in time lost from their sessions. This is especially true in a client's first session, as it results in time lost from developing a therapeutic relationship. Translating at work reminds me of how I did not have the chance to fully be a child—and now I cannot focus fully on being a therapist.

FIRST-GENERATION AND PROUD

I'm sharing my story for other first-generation youth to know they are not alone. Being first-generation is a strength, not a weakness. I hope that young people can find comfort in their experiences and a community to lean on. The guidance and support you receive empowers you to create change and help others. Mentors are important not just professionally, but also emotionally and mentally; when someone validates your experience, you are no longer alone.

Although I grew up as a family interpreter and continue struggling in my adulthood with the challenges of translating for my parents, it further motivates me to advocate. My passion for this issue is at the forefront of my goals as a social worker in ensuring language accessibility in all spaces. Language access is not only ethical, but an investment in all areas of service provision.

I am proud of my intersectionality as a first-generation social worker, woman, Latina, Dominican-American, student, mentor, mentee, advocate, change agent, friend, daughter, sister, cousin, niece, and now author. My journey to self-acceptance comes with a sense of pride for multicultural families, and how despite struggles and systemic barriers, we continue to be resilient through hardship.

Thank you to my madrina Reverend Dr. Jessica Flores for your sponsorship and guidance.

Ancestral Wisdom:

From my mom: "Estoy orgulloso de ver un aumento en el número de intérpretes para personas como yo, pero se necesitan más cambios." (I am proud to see an increase in interpreters for people like me, but more change is needed.)

Journal Prompts

1. How does language access inform your social work journey?
2. Does your experience as a family interpreter relate to internalized beliefs and/or generational trauma?
3. Have you ever been ignored, misunderstood, or ostracized because of the language you speak?
4. How does the importance of community contribute to the healing of trauma?

BIOGRAPHY

Arlys Tineo, LMSW is a native Spanish speaker, social worker, and strong advocate for language access and cultural humility in all spaces. Arlys' passion in the social work field stems from her experiences as a first generation Dominican American. Arlys is currently employed as the Lead Clinician for an unaccompanied minors shelter program at JCCA in Westchester, NY.

Arlys continues to expand her clinical expertise as a part time psychiatric screener/social worker at Good Samaritan Hospital in Suffern, NY, in which she provides psychiatric emergency room screening and supports ED staff with psychiatric and substance use patients.

She is also a member of the Education Committee for the Latino Social Work Coalition.

Arlys received a Bachelor's of Science in Social Work (BSSW) from Medgar Evers College in 2020 and a Master's in Social Work (MSW) from NYU Silver School of Social Work Advanced Standing Program in 2021.

Instagram: arlys_t

Our Trees:
Intergenerational Trauma and Post-Traumatic Growth

ELIZABETH AMADIZ, MSW CANDIDATE

"The thing about these behaviors that stem from a place of pain, a place of trauma, is that typically they don't start with us. These are generational traumas buried, even dormant, within us, but boy once they are activated..."

NUMBNESS

As I sit here today, I haven't cried this much in years. I have sabotaged and procrastinated telling my story for too long. How do we summarize the essence of who we are in a chapter? *Latinx/e in Social Work's* previous authors have been vulnerable and raw; that is scary. Thank you for paving the way. Thank you, to Erica Sandoval and my madrina Madeline Maldonado, for loving me and seeing me even when I didn't do those things for myself.

Social work is a field that can be incredibly rewarding but can constantly drag its finest through the trenches, oftentimes alone. No one really understands the vicarious parts of it, the complex trauma that paves the road to us choosing this field. We aren't here by accident or twisted fate. This field is an unfinished session where we are the ones being assessed, the ones needing the help, needing the difficult conversations, needing to heal the very reasons that delivered us to this field. The truth is that what makes me a great social service provider is that I too struggle every single day. Daily I choose to fight my narrative, to fight my thoughts and my emotions, all while smiling and laughing, all while striving to make a difference so others win their fight. All I can say is I survived.

I survived the aftermath of being sexually assaulted, which is not talked about enough. The toll of assault doesn't end when the attacker leaves. It continues to fester like a malignant heavy mass. The aftermath causes far more damage than most survivors give credit to.

The first time it happened to me, I was 11 or 12 and sitting in the backseat of my parents' car, riding from Santiago to Santo Domingo. In true Dominican fashion we had maybe four or six maletas, so it was a tight ride. My parents were sitting in the front seat and didn't notice his hands reaching over to me. When I felt him touch me, I had no idea what was happening. Not a word nor sound could come out. I simply froze. I was always too afraid to say anything, and I don't remember how I dealt with it after. A lot is still very foggy to me.

This changed the course of my life. Sexual assault, incest, sex—none of these things that clearly happened in previous generations were discussed. This wouldn't be the last time that I just froze. The worst thing is so many people knew about it. There were whispers, I was viewed as promiscuous, and some relationships never recovered as a result. Somehow the warrior in me survived the aftermath. So many years later, I still feel the consequences. Even today I still struggle to accept I was the victim.

The role model women in my family were warriors. Some were forced into loveless marriages, subjected to domestic violence and rape, forced to *aguantar lo imperdonable,* all suffering in silence. These generational ideas of keeping things quiet, keeping the peace, keeping up appearances led many to suffer in the dark. When I think of these women, of my ancestors enduring such pain, I can't help but think of my ancestors who were murdered, raped, and tortured, my ancestors who were robbed of their freedom and how this became normalized, accepted as part of our culture.

Throughout my life, these warriors, my mom and aunts, were the first community workers I ever saw in action. My mother hosted informal back-to-school events. She lent small amounts of money to people and did personal shopping in Chinatown for sheets, curtains, towels, and quilts, all to save money to take things back to her family, such as clothes, notebooks, uniforms, shoes, and so on. My aunts were entrepreneurs, Forbes-level businesswomen who sold pencils, notebooks, sharpeners, flowers, charcoal, ice, and ice cream, owned purperías (like a corner store), pawned household items and clothes, and if you blinked, they may have sold you. But these warriors were surviving and helping others along the way with basic needs. To this day, you can visit my aunts, and they'll help you with a place to stay, medicine, bus fare, and food. These warriors assumed the roles they were dealt and thrived.

Having lived a lifetime before even reaching high school, I was numb. I didn't know how to communicate what I was feeling or what was happening, and I would not know until years later. At that point, I had just learned that my mother was diagnosed with Alzheimer's. I lost her then, though she passed 12 years later. Around that time, I was blessed to meet Ms. Shorter, an amazing social worker who supported me. Through her, I recognized my passion for social work and instantly knew this was where I was meant to be. High school was difficult for me, but Ms. Shorter created a safe space. I realized I wanted to be that safe space for others, but I still had so much to overcome.

HEALING MY INNER CHILD

The baby girl in me, my inner child, survived so much that the adult me didn't know those wounds had become gangrene. I didn't stop to heal those wounds in myself. I kept being of service to others, I kept spreading myself thin. I often chose to turn the other cheek, to procrastinate, to turn up the volume on the negative thoughts and emotional reasoning, while all along helping others to interrupt those narratives.

These unhealed parts of me continuously showed up in my adult relationships, wanting what my inner child yearned for. Oftentimes I worked hard at maintaining, dare I say, dysfunctional relationships with family members, coworkers, friends, and significant others. Waiting for the way I treated others to be contagious enough that it would in turn be the way they loved me. These are some of the ingredients that create people pleasers and lead empathetic souls to fields of service.

The thing about these behaviors that stem from a place of pain, a place of trauma, is that typically they don't start with us. These are generational traumas buried, even dormant, within us, but boy once they are activated… Generations of my ancestors being forced into marriage, being raped, forgoing what they felt to be love all *por el nombre de la familia, por el que dirán.* Today I have social work to thank for being able to gain a deeper understanding of myself, for teaching me that research shows we carry between seven and 14 generations of trauma within us. How ironic that when this begins to seep out of our pores, we are labeled as our behaviors, our symptoms of something that doesn't even belong to us.

Sadly, most of the warriors I mentioned, my silent role models, are no longer with us. Many of them swallowed their trauma, which turned poisonous, morphing into brain aneurysms, cancer, dementia, Alzheimer's—all trauma symptomatic. I stand here today, saying it has to end with us. We have to use these chapters, these volumes, and our access to treat the underlying traumas of our generations to heal those wounds.

Working over 13 years in this field, I just kept going, overextending, people-pleasing, and being available for everyone. 2020 broke me; I suffered in silence. But eventually I was forced to unpack it all. I kept getting referred sexual assault cases of young girls, including one who was being trafficked whose family didn't believe her. I was dreaming about these kids. Going through my own stuff. Feeling stuck. Working during the COVID-19 pandemic just heightened my depression and anxiety. I was at the darkest place again shortly after I got help.

This has taught me that those things we put on the back burner, using busy bee syndrome—when we don't deal with it, sit with it, and acknowledge it—eventually grow too heavy for us to continue carrying and we are forced to deal with it. Even as a mental health professional, I didn't realize I had been suffering from PTSD. Therapy saved my life. I am here to say it is okay to say no, to walk away from jobs, to prioritize ourselves, to put that oxygen mask on first, to take that respite.

I made the hard decision to quit my job with no safety net, no plan B, no savings—just the desire to get better. While I have an amazing support system, the problem wasn't exterior but interior. Breaking down stigma begins with us. Many communities are quick to treat hypertension, cholesterol, and diabetes, but postpone or stigmatize mental health. I'm here to educate my community. I want to normalize community conversations around sexual assault, mental health, and access to care because even for me it was a struggle to secure a provider. Social work can look very different; you can become a macro, mezzo, or micro social worker, or better yet all of the above. I know I will make a difference; this is my purpose. I made it out of the darkness, and I'm ready to shine.

Ancestral Wisdom:

Mis tías would say, "Hay que hacer de tripas, corazones." Translation: Look for the beauty within the difficult times.

Journal Prompts:
1. If you could write a letter to one of your ancestors, what would you say as you release your intergenerational trauma?
2. Write your own ancestral wisdom to be passed down to future generations.
3. As you continue in your healing journey, what do you see yourself doing to support your community with the same lived experience?

BIOGRAPHY

Elizabeth Amadiz is an MSW candidate and a passionate community educator focused on mental health awareness. She actively participates in community events, providing education to normalize conversations about mental health and encourage seeking care. On social media, Elizabeth engages her audience by discussing crucial topics like self-care and self-awareness.

Born and raised in Crown Heights, Brooklyn, Elizabeth witnessed firsthand the challenges faced by disproportionate communities, which inspired her to dedicate over a decade to serving primarily Latinx populations. Her mission is to change the perception of mental health, advocating for it to be recognized as an integral part of overall health.

Elizabeth is committed to helping families and communities have open, stigma-free conversations about mental well-being, just as they would with any other health issue. She strives to destigmatize mental health and eliminate the taboos that often accompany it, fostering a culture where accessing care is prioritized and normalized.

RISING FROM THE ASHES

JACQUELINE AVILES-TORRES, MSW, LSW, SSW

"The collapse of my intergenerational trauma bridge ended when I rose from the ashes like a phoenix."

THE UNWANTED ONE

Me recuerdo de estas palabras que me dijeron varios miembros de mi familia extendida: "¡Tú Madre era muy cabrita y tu saliste a ella!" At the ripe age of three, I could never understand what my family meant by this phrase, but the constant reminder that I was the unwanted one was always very clear throughout my journey. As an Afro-Latina Puerto Rican female born to a 15-year-old mom, the odds were stacked against me from the moment my mother got pregnant.

To this day I ask myself, "Why did she have me?" My biological father had already begun physically, verbally, emotionally, and financially abusing my exotically beautiful and very talented young mother before I was even conceived. I was the product of rape and domestic violence, and I was reminded constantly that I didn't originate from love. A "super preemie," I weighed less than four pounds when I was born, my mother giving birth at barely six months pregnant. She often told me that I could fit in her hand, and I wondered why she kept me.

Extended family members fed me stories blaming my mother for the abuse she endured after meeting this monster of a father and husband. As a toddler, I witnessed him put out cigarettes on my mother's back and shoulders and how he blamed her for not being good enough. This monster even stated that he wanted a son, a son who my mother wasn't good enough to bear because all she produced was garbage. He made it very clear to me that my mother was beaten and punished for my existence. He would make an example out of her in front of others as he beat her, dragging, punching, and kicking her in the head, back, and stomach, biting her arms and thighs until the floor was wet with her blood.

THE FIRE

During one night of his drunken and drugged up moments, he duct taped my mother to a chair and told me he would free me from my garbage, poor excuse of a mother. "Today she dies, and you will go with her!" he yelled. My body became frozen and numb. I couldn't move. I couldn't cry. I remember the urine dripping down the sides of my legs as my mother fought back, and by the grace of the almighty, the chair she was strapped to fell and shattered. Mustering all of her strength, my mother crawled to me and collapsed.

After her collapse, my biological father left, and I thought, "The monster is gone, my mom is breathing… we are finally free!" But this was just the beginning of the end. I still remember the odor of blood, urine, and beer mixed with the pungent smell of my biological father's shirt as my three-year-old hands worked to free my mother as he attempted to burn us alive. As I scurried and tried to get my mom to wake up, my biological father was outside dowsing the entrance of our small apartment door with gasoline, and the moment he lit the match, I thought this was truly the end for us. But we miraculously escaped.

NEW BEGINNINGS

After several months in a shelter, my mother and I left Boston to move to Newark, New Jersey, and I remember admiring my mother, her beauty and resilience. I felt that although it was just the two of us that this was enough for me. Finally, we would be around people who would take care of and love us. But that wasn't the case—we were back on the "hamster wheel" of intergenerational trauma. Again, our family verbally abused my mother, blaming her for what had happened to her. I watched as my mother was reprimanded by elders, and though I tried to be brave for her, I couldn't get it right, I couldn't fix it, I couldn't fix her, I couldn't help us!

Sadly, my beloved mother also became my abuser, as I was a direct reminder of my father, her abuser. At the time, I thought I deserved the baseball bat strikes to my head and body, the visits to the emergency room, the broken nose, the broken bones, the bruises, and my broken self. I deserved it all. I was the reason for her abuse, and our family made sure I would never forget it.

When I was seven, my mother tried to take breaks from seeing me and sent me to sleep over with family members. I didn't know what it was to have a childhood nor what it was to be welcomed and accepted. No matter how my mother processed her trauma, all I knew was that she was all I had, and she was the glimmer of my eyes. But those sleepovers led to seven years of molestation and verbal, physical, and sexual abuse by those who were supposed to be a positive part of my life. It was during these years that I lost all of myself. I became a punching bag and an object of sexual exploitation. But it was in our culture to keep quiet about the abuse and to normalize all that had happened to my mother, me, and other family members. While I was away with family, mom entered a new relationship, which created two new additions, my talented brother and my beautiful sister. They became the joys of my life, and even at my young age, I knew I had to try to protect them at any cost.

When I was 15, my mother sent me away to Puerto Rico, a place I would fall in love with—my culture, my island, the land of my people. I soon realized that my mother wouldn't come back for me, and although I endured additional abuse, including rape, and was grieving being taken away from my nuclear family, I understood that no one would save me. It was literally "do or die" and "become a statistic," or claw my way out of the intergenerational cultural trauma and succeed.

I had to learn how to survive on $25 a month while living with extended family members who yanked my childhood away from me. I made sure to take care of myself as I finished high school in a place that also discriminated against me—I hadn't been American enough in America, and now I wasn't Afro-Latina/Puerto Rican enough in Puerto Rico. But I chose to keep learning how to turn my intergenerational cultural trauma, pain, anger, and resentment into the fuel I needed to succeed. I worked hard, became one with my island, learned about our history, and while attending the university in Rio Piedras, I got involved in political movements to help address impoverished communities' need for housing. Although my relationship with my mother wasn't picture perfect, she was enough for me, and I was enough for her to the point that she chose to die in my arms, saying she loved me and transitioning as I cradled her on Mother's Day.

REFLECTION

Although this is only about a quarter of my story, in spite of all the "trials and tribulations," I endured. My strength, my faith, my nuclear family, and my resilience catapulted me to yet more years of learning that I am the agent of my own change and that this intergenerational cultural trauma would end with me by healing the woman, leader, and married queer mother of two amazing children who I have become. For years I was told that I wasn't good enough and would amount to nothing. Anything and everything you could imagine, I have endured and survived. I have survived my own horrors and turned them into my victories. I am not my tragedy nor my trauma. The collapse of my intergenerational trauma bridge ended when I rose from the ashes like a phoenix.

As a licensed social worker and first-generation graduate, I didn't become a statistic. And as I continue with my clinical career, on my Ifa/Yorubian faith journey, prioritizing myself, forgiving, and healing, I have come to understand that my trauma has helped strengthen my abilities to trust my intuition that I am not my trauma or just another label.

I invite you to trust and reflect on your process and your own journey. Although it is easier said than done, know that you are enough and that you deserve to never give up on yourself. I honor you and invite you to validate your journey because that's how you view and mold your experiences into serving your higher sense of self. As you reflect on your journey, be mindful and kind with yourself, starting with the journal prompts below.

Ancestral Wisdom

You are not alone even in your darkest experiences. Take a moment, breathe in, and realize that you are armed with ancestral insight, which makes you an unstoppable force.

Journal Prompts:

1. How hard is it for you to validate your journey?
2. Can you put a name to what has catapulted you to who you have become today?
3. How do you honor your journey? And if you don't, do

you believe you are capable of becoming your own hero?

BIOGRAPHY

Jacqueline Aviles-Torres is a first-generation university graduate who has served over 25 years in the field of social work.

Jacqueline takes great pride in representing her community. Although she has worked most of her professional career in New Jersey, she is now expanding her work to New York City to serve undocumented and underserved populations, focusing on Latinx communities. Her purpose is to be a leader, advocate, and voice for those that are unheard and feel invisible in this country.

Jacqueline is the founder of Core Family Solutions LLC, which will be the continued foundation of her therapeutic and overall services.

Corefamilysolutions@gmail.com
LinkedIn: www.linkedin.com/in/jacqueline-a-6838b057

CHARISMA

EVELYN BAUTISTA-MILLER, LMSW, SDA, SIFI

"I did everything that Mami modeled, just bilingually."

TRANSFORMING LIVES: A SOCIAL WORKER'S JOURNEY IN YOUTH EMPOWERMENT

"Evelyn, vámonos!"

I had heard this phrase ever since I was seven years old from my late mother, Isabel Bautista, an immigrant from San Francisco de Macorís, Dominican Republic. Out of all of us—my three older siblings, twin brother, and younger sister—I would most frequently accompany her to social service agencies to interpret on her behalf. Since my mother was an entrepreneur, I would also go as her interpreter to sell and collect monies owed to her within the neighborhood.

My mother would rotate us as her interpreter in these spaces to ensure that one did not miss more school than the other, but I frequently went. She always described me as the type of child who enjoyed being outside and interacting with others. I always looked forward to a conversation with someone new and was both socially and emotionally perceptive. She said that I was *muy simpática:* I was naturally charming and charismatic. As I got older, I realized it was my charisma that served as her secret weapon at these agencies. I was the cute kid who revealed her dimples every time she smiled, which was often, and had a big personality with big black curly hair to match. She realized early on that all of these things would soften the often challenging interactions between her and English-speaking caseworkers, especially when some grew frustrated with the fact that she only spoke Spanish. I was there to not just interpret, but charm and sweeten these conversations so that we received necessary support.

Not every experience was always ideal, as I witnessed at a young age how unkind people can be when a language barrier presents itself. When I was eleven years old, I was interpreting for my mother at the welfare office and the caseworker was not being kind to us. While I don't remember the specifics of the interaction, I do remember that the caseworker asked for a certain set of documents, and my mother had a few questions about those documents and the overall process. I remember interpreting my mother's questions as the caseworker's comments evolved from abrupt to openly disrespectful. I had experience with how to diffuse a situation when caseworkers became unkind—which happened a lot—but I did not have experience when they became cruel. At one point, the caseworker made a comment referencing both the amount of children that my mother had and our paternity in a manner that was so unnecessarily cruel that I immediately stopped interpreting and said, "I'm sorry. Do you *really* want me to say that to my mom?"

We locked eyes as she paused, and though brief, that moment felt like an eternity. I truly believe that in this moment, she realized that even though she was in conversation with an adult, I, a child, also heard everything that she had uttered. Her responses became less abrupt as we continued, but I felt hurt that this was my mother's experience. Because she did not speak English, she was often treated as if she was less intelligent and less deserving of support in these spaces. As a child, these interactions were uncomfortable for me, as I heard people say a lot of unkind things about my mother in my presence. Even though I would not interpret unkind remarks, I believe Mami could tell when they occurred. I cannot imagine how having these interactions in the presence of her child affected her.

Being charismatic did not feel like anything special because I did everything that my mother stood for. She was one of the most charming and charismatic people I knew. She had the gift of gab, and was very compassionate and community-oriented. She cared deeply about our neighborhood and counseled everyone who was in need of advice. When someone passed away, she would bring homemade meals to their loved ones during their time of grief.

She would make *sancocho* for people in our neighborhood who were having a hard time emotionally or financially. She was so revered in our community that a local priest was able to extend an offer of admission for me and my siblings to attend a prestigious Catholic school in the South Bronx. I did everything that Mami modeled, just bilingually.

These experiences shaped me and the way that I viewed the world, especially regarding language accessibility in institutions and public agencies. Since I was a child, I had been curating an ability to connect Spanish speakers with important resources thanks to my charismatic approach. I had learned how to make meaningful connections with people from all walks of life and across different identities. When I left my hometown of the Bronx for college, I knew that whatever path I chose, I was going to help others with my ability to speak Spanish.

SOCIAL WORK ODYSSEY: A JOURNEY OF PURPOSE

I firmly believe that when you manifest your purpose, God will introduce you to the people and experiences that will reinforce it. I was fortunate enough to be accepted into the prestigious social work program at SUNY-Albany. During my time there, I was connected to the chief of the campus police force, who later became a mentor of mine. Once, he saw me on campus and greeted me with a nickname that he still calls me to this day: "Charisma." While we had spoken about my life in the South Bronx growing up, I never shared with him the private conversation about charisma I'd had with my mother. He explained that he called me that because I exude positive energy all the time, and he believed my aura to be a gift from God. Perhaps my mother knew this as well and saw it in me at an early age. Perhaps she saw a God-given talent in me that she knew I needed to curate.

Attending SUNY-Albany was one of the best decisions I ever made, as the experiences I had there really helped set the foundation for the life that I would ultimately lead. I was able to develop my leadership skills by joining Zeta Phi Beta Sorority, Inc., Epsilon Nu Chapter which is a historically Black Greek letter organization. I then joined Fuerza Latina, a campus affinity group for students of Latin American descent and open to all. I also joined the UAlbany Pan Hellenic Council, the umbrella organization for sororities and fraternities, and served as a Vice President. Joining these organizations really helped me become more comfortable in my own skin because I was able to find spaces that affirmed both of my identities as an Afro-Latina while also developing community leadership skills. I learned how to fundraise, coordinate large events, and recruit people to join organizations. My sorority and other campus activities taught me how to become a servant leader for the community, something that I believe all skilled social workers are. Like Mami said, I have never met a person that I was not interested in building rapport and conversing with. I did not realize that my entire life, Mami was setting me up to develop empathetic leadership skills.

I know it sounds cliché, but one day, we all wake up and the sayings that our parents told us just make sense. In these moments, we realize that our parents have been preparing us for experiences we would face later in our lives. For me, that moment happened in graduate school. I was in a discussion with my classmates during my Social Welfare course and we had such a great dialogue about the lesson. I had an amazing professor who made me (and other classmates) feel so safe and heard when sharing our lived experiences. I remember being in that course and learning the vocabulary to describe skills that I had already possessed. Because I did not previously have the academic language to describe aspects of my personality, I did not realize just how valuable being charismatic could be professionally, especially in the field of social work. It was affirming to finally receive formal education atop the informal training that Mami provided.

By the time I left Albany, I had a Master of Social Work (MSW) and was ready to take on the world. My first job post-graduate school was as a supervisor at a foster care agency. It was impactful work, as I witnessed just how much support foster children need from their schools. I did not stay in this role long because I knew that I needed to be a school social worker, to help all students thrive and be successful. I wanted to be in a space where I could make the most impact on youth, and it made sense to be in an institution where children spend the majority of their time.

THE CHARISMATIC HERITAGE: FROM CHILDHOOD TO LEADERSHIP

As someone who has interpreted for others throughout my career, I often think of my many experiences interpreting for my mother. As a social worker, I realized that my mother's communication gaps with social services did not stem from the fact that she did not speak English. I saw her speak to everyone in our community. She was a counselor, advisor, and advocate who never had an issue speaking her mind. The true issue was that these agencies and schools did not speak Spanish. As a person in need of services, this operational lapse burdened her.

I am fortunate to disrupt this obstacle for so many others as a school social worker. I have witnessed Spanish-speaking parents and guardians breathe a sigh of relief when they can communicate with me in Spanish. Because of who I am and who I was raised to be, they can engage with my school in a way that was once inaccessible. I see them on Back to School Nights and other school events; they feel comfortable calling me to schedule meetings with administrators and educators to discuss their child's academic goals and emotional well-being. There's an entire population that I am helping my district serve that has historically gone ignored.

Though I completed a competitive social work program and have several licenses and certifications, I believe that with her second-grade education, my mother Isabel Bautista taught me how to be an effective and compassionate social worker. Many other first-generation children have similar stories interpreting for their family members. Charisma is nothing but the ability to build and sustain personal connections with others, and I went with her everywhere to learn how to do that.

Reader, I am here to remind you to be charismatic in all that you do. Because of my mother and my charisma, I developed a skill set that has helped me become an award-winning and state-recognized social worker, now able to improve language access for parents and children in my community.

Ancestral Wisdom:

Recuerda siempre de dónde vienes, porque allí encontrarás la fuerza para seguir adelante. (Always remember where you come from, for there you will find the strength to keep moving forward.)

Journal Prompts:
1. What non-academic or "soft" skills do you possess that strengthen your role in social work?
2. How has your background or cultural identity impacted how you serve others?
3. Does your experience as a family interpreter connect to internalized beliefs and/or generational trauma?

BIOGRAPHY

Evelyn Bautista-Miller is a bilingual Certified Licensed Social Worker (LMSW) & School District Administrator in NY and NJ.

In 2014, Bautista-Miller founded the non-profit Tender Steps of New York, Inc. (TSONY, Inc.). As President, she oversees TSONY's work to meet unmet social needs while advocating with legislators for more inclusive policies.

Bautista-Miller is a graduate of the Rockefeller School of Social Welfare at SUNY-Albany, and is currently completing her Ph.D. in Social Welfare from CUNY-Graduate Center.

To learn more about Bautista-Miller and TSONY, Inc., please visit www.tenderstepsofny.org/

FROM MARGINS TO MOMENTUM: MY SOCIAL WORK JOURNEY THROUGH SYSTEMIC SHADOWS

CRISTINO N. CHAVEZ JR., LMSW, CTP

"You can jail a Revolutionary, but you can't jail the Revolution."
—Fred Hampton, American Civil Rights Leader & Deputy Chairman of the Black Panther Party, Illinois

PART ONE: MARGINS

Imagine if I proposed the idea that our criminal justice system isn't actually broken, but deliberately crafted to marginalize and oppress communities of color—would that resonate with you? And what if I shared that I've personally navigated the biases within this system—would it alter your perception of me?

These thoughts often cross my mind during walks along the path to the subway station behind the Parkchester Condominiums, where the surrounding natural beauty and tall trees swaying in the breeze invite introspection into my personal life and the traumas I've experienced. It's in moments like these that I wonder deeply about my life's direction. How did I transition from being handcuffed behind a police car to sitting at my desk, typing my narrative for others to read? Why did I choose social work, and what drove me to turn my past into a force for change today?

Since the start of colonization, my ancestors strived and survived through ongoing genocide and plagues that nearly wiped away the entire indigenous population. They continued to strive and survive from the Salvadoran Civil War to immigration policies that impact millions of indigenous people originating from Latin America. My ancestors taught me to acknowledge my worth and to remember that every moment in your life serves a purpose in your journey. From surviving in a toxic, colonized environment to gaining my independence and having the freedom to express myself, I take pride in the work I do, the moments of growth, the sacrifices I've made, the lessons I've learned, and the activism I experience as a macro social worker.

Growing up in Glen Cove as a first-generation Salvadoran, my childhood felt like a balancing act between embracing who I was and seizing the joys of youth amidst a backdrop of struggle and constraint. My life was a constant tug of war. On one side, there was the rich tapestry of my Salvadoran heritage and the tight-knit community that came with it. On the other were the harsh realities of growing up in a suburban town tinged with racism and bound by rigid religious expectations that didn't leave much room for the carefree exploration of youth.

School was a battleground where I endured bullying, not just for my ethnicity but for the earnestness with which I approached my responsibilities at home, my dedication to the church, my efforts to excel academically, and my part-time job as a busboy. My every action seemed to invite criticism, which over time turned into a chorus of self-doubt that criticized every step I took, pushing me to strive for unattainable perfection instead of recognizing the value of my best efforts.

Amidst this turmoil, I grappled with my identity, carrying the weight of being gay in an environment where homophobic slurs were as common as the air I breathed. Each joke, each denial I uttered in response, only deepened the internal scars of guilt and self-reproach.

And then, as if adolescence wasn't challenging enough, I was diagnosed with a brain tumor. This new battle brought its own set of fears and challenges, yet it was just another layer added to the complex web of my life's struggles—struggles that included translating for my family and navigating the labyrinth of paperwork that our life in the United States entailed.

Looking back, I realize how these experiences shaped me, even as they threatened to break me. They taught me resilience, compassion, and the true meaning of strength—not the strength to reach some artificial standard of perfection, but the strength to accept myself and my efforts as enough, even in the face of adversity and misunderstanding.

High school is a period many reminisce about as the golden years, filled with fond memories and firsts. However, for me, those years were overshadowed by challenges, despite my deep love for learning and education. On graduation day, I was already looking ahead, determined to seize every opportunity for personal growth. I dreamed of living independently in a big city, where I could freely express myself as a first-generation Salvadoran and a gay man.

PART TWO: MOMENTUM

Entering my freshman year at SUNY Old Westbury, I felt a mix of gratitude and excitement. I was determined to make my undergraduate years count, to make them the best of my life. And for the most part, I succeeded, soaking in every moment of learning and growth. However, there was a pivotal experience that profoundly shifted my perspective on life.

Throughout these years, I often found myself pondering the depths of the justice system, especially as it impacted my own family. My visits to the Nassau County Correctional Center, where I saw loved ones behind bars, left me questioning: How does it feel to walk in their shoes? This curiosity wasn't just academic; it was deeply personal. My job at a mental health nonprofit as a care coordinator only expanded my interest in the experiences of those entangled in the justice system.

Then, one warm April night changed everything. After reuniting with friends and indulging in a few drinks, I made a decision that would alter the course of my life. Intoxicated, I got behind the wheel in the Bronx, believing I could safely drive home. But in just seconds, my car collided with another vehicle, which had passengers inside, and a police car was immediately on the scene. The moment the sirens flashed, I was engulfed in the crushing realization that my life, as I knew it, might be over.

Sitting handcuffed in the backseat after failing a breathalyzer test, the weight of my actions crashed down on me. Thoughts of losing my cherished job, the chance to advance my education in a Master of Social Work program, and other future opportunities in my field swirled in my mind like a relentless storm. It wasn't until I was standing before the judge at my arraignment that a glimmer of hope pierced through the despair. In that moment, I drew strength from memories of my work as a care coordinator, recalling how I had supported clients entangled in the justice system, helping them rebuild their lives piece by piece.

Miraculously, I managed to graduate and retain my job, a relief that was overshadowed by a profound realization. Through my own brush with the justice system, I became acutely aware of the trauma and the stark lack of support faced by those who have been labeled as "criminals." This experience reshaped my mission in life. I was determined more than ever to challenge and change the very system that continues to oppress the people and communities I hold dear. My journey through the system, albeit brief, ignited a passion to advocate for those caught within its grasp, to ensure they receive the support and understanding they desperately need.

Embarking on my MSW journey as a part-time student

meant navigating a reality where my time was split between a full-time job, 21 hours of weekly field placement, and responsibilities as a graduate and research assistant. Initially, I was drawn to exploring how my personal encounters with the criminal justice system could enrich my clinical practice. However, everything changed the day I started my course on social welfare and policies. This course shifted my career focus to macro social work. I became deeply interested in tackling the systemic issues within our criminal justice system, aiming to make a difference through research and policy advocacy.

Over the next three years, I immersed myself in community service and actively participated in various academic and county-based councils and committees. These platforms allowed me to address and challenge the current practices that disproportionately affect Black, Brown, Latino, and immigrant communities across New York City and Long Island. My graduation from the MSW program in 2019, followed by obtaining my LMSW in 2020, marked the beginning of a new chapter. Armed with my degree, license, and a wealth of hands-on experience, I felt fully equipped to step into the social justice sector. My mission was clear: to advocate for criminal and juvenile justice reform, immigration, and child welfare, aiming to dismantle the systemic barriers that hinder equity and justice.

REFLECTION

Reflecting on my journey, I've come to realize how my personal trauma stemming from an encounter with the criminal justice system has profoundly shaped my career, ignited my passion, and defined my purpose in life. Growing up, I often felt ensnared within my community, grappling with harassment at school and the scars of religious trauma, all of which erected formidable barriers in my path. This sense of entrapment was compounded by habitual self-criticism, to the extent that fear of rejection led me to apply to only one university for my undergraduate studies. The initial rejection from that university felt like confirmation of my deepest fears, but with encouragement and support, that decision was reversed to an acceptance, fueling my resolve to persevere.

This resilience has transformed me into someone I once thought impossible to become: a proud Salvadoran social worker with a career that once seemed like a distant dream. My journey from a case manager during my undergraduate days to a licensed social worker and doctoral student pursuing a PhD in Social Work has been nothing short of extraordinary. Today, I juggle roles as a research associate, an adjunct professor at NYU Silver School of Social Work, and an immigration court mental health consultant, all while being deeply involved in civic engagement.

Navigating my journey from being arrested to the tense atmosphere of a court sentence hearing, I've come face-to-face with the stark realities of trauma resulting from police interactions and the courtroom. These experiences laid bare the profound injustices that communities of color endure, injustices that not only scar but also stifle their chances for healing and advancement. There were moments I struggled with imposter syndrome, questioning my qualifications to serve in the capacities I do today as a social worker. I would often wonder if I truly belonged in these roles, only to be reminded of the numerous rejections and hurdles I faced across various facets of my life—professional, academic, and personal. Yet, these challenges never deterred me. Instead, they fueled my resolve to push through, to seek mental health treatment for my own traumas, and to find strength in the support and guidance of others. Now, as I stand in the roles of a social worker, research associate, PhD student, adjunct professor, and immigration court mental health evaluator, my commitment to the community and my love for what I do grow ever stronger. Each step I take in my professional journey is a step towards lighting a beacon of hope for those who fear they might not see tomorrow.

Social work has opened doors to incredible opportunities, allowing me to advocate for criminal justice reform—a cause deeply personal to me, especially after my arrest. It has endowed me with the hope and determination to actively contribute to my community, to support those who are vulnerable and to stand against the injustices we face together. My journey underscores the transformative power of social work, not just in the lives of those we serve but in the very essence of who we become as practitioners and advocates in the fight for justice and equity.

Understanding the layers of personal and intergenerational trauma that have shaped me, acknowledging the pivotal decisions of my life, and recognizing the growth stemming from self-belief have all guided me towards social work. It's here, in this field, that I've found my calling to champion the causes of criminal justice reform, juvenile justice reform, immigration, and civil rights. Inspired by Dr. Martin Luther King Jr.'s words, "Injustice anywhere is a threat to justice everywhere," I've dedicated myself to a personal mission—a mission to dismantle oppressive systems, challenge injustices both locally and nationally, and promote restorative justice. This journey is about creating spaces where we can all live, grow, and thrive, embodying the belief that amidst our collective striving for success, each of us has the potential to make a significant impact.

Ancestral Wisdom:

Mi mami: "Reconoce la fuerza que tienes y nunca te olvides." (Recognize the strength you have and never forget.)

Journal Prompts:
1. Have personal experiences with the criminal justice system influenced your interest in social work?
2. Has there been a definitive "turning point" in your journey?
3. How can you make a difference in criminal justice reform?

BIOGRAPHY

Cristino N. Chavez Jr. is a Licensed Master Social Worker (LMSW) and Certified Trauma Professional (CTP) and is currently an Adjunct Professor at the New York University Silver School of Social Work, as well as an Immigration Court Mental Health Evaluator. Cristino received his BA in Psychology at SUNY Old Westbury and his MSW at Adelphi University School of Social Work. Cristino is currently enrolled as a Doctoral Student at Yeshiva University Wurzweiler School of Social Work on his journey toward earning his Ph.D. in Social Welfare. His focus in research, policy, and clinical practice includes criminal and juvenile justice, immigration, gang and gun violence, restorative justice, government, politics and law, mass incarceration, and criminal justice reform.

EMBRACING IDENTITY: A NEUROSPICY TALE

SANDRA N. CRESPO, LICSW

"ADHD, like any superpower, requires understanding, management, and intentionality to harness its powerful potential."

ROOTS

Camuy, a sun-drenched town nestled on Puerto Rico's northwest coast, served as the backdrop of my childhood. It was a tapestry of cultural richness and familial love. Surrounded by cousins and rooted in a humble yet vibrant community, I thrived without the weight of the world's problems. Raised by my mother, of Syrian and Cuban descent, and my Puerto Rican father, I was immersed in a blend of colors, traditions, music, language, and art. I still remember the chill that would run up my spine when I'd step on the grass with its morning dew, el rocio de la mañana. Qué bello empezar el día con tanta paz.

From an early age, I sensed my differences. Dubbed "Nahir Sufrimiento" by my uncles for my easily stirred emotions, I discovered I was born an empath, deeply feeling the world around me. Nature became my sanctuary, animals my companions, books and art my solace. I'd spend countless hours outside, lost in books or watching insects crawl up leaves and stones, birds hopping from tree to tree, lagartijos slithering in and out of sight. I was a perpetual daydreamer, fascinated by everything. Driven by curiosity, my penchant for questioning often clashed with the "do as you're told" expectation, yet my thirst for knowledge led me to academic acceleration — reading and writing by age four, sketching and painting even earlier, all nurtured by my mother. A Latina mother, the product of an ever-layered combination of her own joys and trauma, saw her firstborn's peculiarities as strengths and nurtured them through storytelling and fashion. I am so very grateful.

Energetic and eager, my parents immersed me in endless activities—photography, modeling, gymnastics, sports, dance, piano, art classes—believing busyness equaled worth. I spearheaded "booked and busy." I fell in love with learning, any subject a rabbit hole of discovery. I was the 10-year-old listening to my uncles talk about politics, completely taken aback at how the idea of "government" worked. I wondered why my titis all married so young, why they didn't leave to see the world first. I didn't seem to want what most kids wanted; I wanted freedom, even without fully understanding its meaning. I challenged rules and frequently asked "why not?" My oddness was welcomed and fed with inclusion and safety. It was my launching pad.

Life felt limitless until my parents' divorce shattered our Puerto Rican idyll. In 1999, my mother abruptly uprooted us to Boston. I faced a daunting new chapter where English ruled and integration posed formidable challenges. I became angry at my mother for separating me and my siblings from my father. There was so much I despised about our new home, beginning with its brutal winter temperatures and its lack of seasoned food—because what is shepherd's pie?? Dios mío! Everything felt wrong.

UN FRÍO VIOLENTO

In Boston, I faced the stark reality of language barriers and cultural adaptation head-on. Unfamiliar with English but determined to prove myself, I deep-dove into English books, music, and television, meticulously refining my pronunciation to soften my accent. Just like anything else I've ever set my mind to, I pursued it relentlessly. I couldn't fail. I couldn't miss. My mother decided against enrolling me in English as a second language (ESL) classes because "no vinimos a los Estados Unidos para hablar español, aprende y domina," and that I did.

School remained my sanctuary, with art class becoming my refuge. Through my high school art teacher, I began to explore self-awareness and the power of the mind, learning to harness my whirlwind of thoughts with sketching. I grappled with a short attention span and procrastination, struggling with day-to-day tasks and maintaining connections outside my immediate circle. Exhaustion became a constant companion as I pushed myself relentlessly, always equating productivity with self-worth and resisting rest, a perceived waste of time. I couldn't stop.

Despite these challenges, I excelled in high school and dominated English class. I attended Suffolk University, initially pursuing a criminal justice major, driven by a vague interest in law enforcement. Halfway through, I switched to sociology. This decision was directly influenced by my first unintentional job in social work. I was hired at a non-profit as a "therapeutic mentor," working with self-harming young girls. I knew nothing about therapy, but I was all too familiar with internal chaos. Instinctively, I knew these girls lacked the words to describe their pain, and even if they had the words, I wanted to introduce them to alternative forms of expression, as my art teacher had done with me. I began introducing non-verbal techniques for connection. Art, photography, poetry, hiking—all ways to connect to themselves without searching for words. The world could wait; the real goal was for them to understand themselves. Through this, I learned the power of silence, a long-term contributor to my identity both as an individual and a professional.

My journey continued with a Master of Social Work, where I incorrectly but unknowingly embraced my quirks as integral to my personality. I was excelling academically but failing in my personal life. Losing friendships and being criticized for forgetting important dates and deadlines led me to gravitate toward "low-maintenance" relationships, oddly shaping my social circle and alienating genuine friendships that I later learned were a mistake to ignore.

It was, however, during my MSW studies that I discovered a passion for leadership, coinciding with my promotion to a managerial role in Child Protective Services. Realizing my challenges wouldn't disappear, I developed personal tools like color-coded calendars and thousands of sticky notes to manage my memory and follow-through—bulletproof methods, of course! But I continued to struggle with my identity. Was I good enough to be a leader? Imposter syndrome became a toxic, loyal friend, and I struggled day in and day out to find my "why."

Under the guidance of my first supportive mentor, I learned leadership frameworks rooted in empathy and accountability, nurturing my passion for leadership development and revealing a path beyond conventional molds. This pivotal moment in my career solidified my commitment to advocating for others and fostering growth within teams.

UN CALOR AMOROSO

In 2018, an opportunity arose for me to work within executive leadership in the Washington, DC, city government via the Capital City Fellowship Program. This program laid the groundwork for what turned out to be a beautiful ascension into what my career is today.

As I navigated various leadership roles in my social work career, it was my position as vice president of operations at a cybersecurity company that prompted profound self-reflection. Exhausted by the demands of social work, I decided to switch professions, believing a change would better suit my cognitive style, although I still didn't fully understand it. In my role as VP, I realized I had yet to adequately address my own needs or fully integrate the leadership training I had accumulated. I began experiencing frequent mental blocks—I struggled with focus and basic tasks, and my overall performance suffered. I was completely burnt out. Days would pass without me eating or drinking simply because I forgot. This baffled those around me who suggested I just needed a better organizational system, despite my exhaustive efforts to find one. It seemed like nothing worked.

It was during this challenging period that I started reading about neurodivergence, specifically ADHD. As I delved deeper, I felt an overwhelming sense of recognition. The descriptions I read mirrored my personality, shortcomings, quirks, and strengths perfectly—they provided an explanation for everything I had struggled with. After consulting with my doctor, I received confirmation—I was indeed an ADHDer or, as I like to call it, NeuroSpicy!

This realization was transformative. Embracing my neurodivergent identity as a visionary and strategist, I embarked on a journey of intense personal development. Through self-reflection and a relentless pursuit of understanding, I unearthed strengths in listening, processing information, and leading with empathy—a shift that turned perceived challenges into unique advantages. Embracing my identity as a neurodivergent Latina leader brought clarity and relief, shaping my leadership style to prioritize compassion—a NeuroSpicy approach!

This journey also illuminated the importance of creating supportive environments tailored to individual needs in leadership, friendships, and partnerships. It deepened my understanding of workplace dynamics and the diversity of the human experience. ADHD, like any superpower, requires understanding, management, and intentionality to harness its powerful potential. It's an integral part of who I am, empowering me to advocate for neurodiversity as a valuable perspective rather than a limitation. Throughout my journey, I realized that non-verbal modalities in working with NeuroSpicy clients can be incredibly effective not only in fostering connection, but also in encouraging healthy expression.

I can only hope that sharing my story empowers people from all walks of life to embrace their uniqueness and pursue career paths aligned with their strengths. As a proud NeuroSpicy Latina leader, I am passionate about raising awareness and creating inclusive spaces that celebrate diversity. This led me to create Unalome Consulting Group (UCG), an organization that focuses on inclusive leadership development and coaching with a unique neurodivergent lens. My current role as clinic director for a multidisciplinary mental health practice provides me with an amazing platform to implement an inclusive and compassionate leadership framework, resulting in higher retention and quality productivity. I finally found my why; I found my purpose.

Thank you to my mentors Dr. Anthony Estreet, Fabienne Pierre, and Erica Priscilla Sandoval.

Ancestral Wisdom:

My Tío always said there is beauty in the breakdown. If something is breaking down, it means it needs to change. It is a rebirth.

Journal Prompts:

1. What is your understanding of neurodivergence? How has your understanding shaped your interactions with people that are "NeuroSpicy?"
2. If you are neurodivergent, how has it proven challenging and/or rewarding?
3. What are some of your superpowers?

BIOGRAPHY

Sandra N. Crespo is a licensed clinical social worker, professor, and advocate for diversity in social work leadership. As Clinic Director for Transformations Care Network in the DMV region, she integrates technology with clinical therapy for inclusive mental health care. Sandra founded Unalome Consulting Group (UCG) to coach and nurture leaders, focusing on the LatinX and Neurodivergent communities. Her career includes clinical practice, program design, and executive administration in Child Protective Services and Juvenile Justice in Massachusetts, Maryland, and Washington, D.C. A Neurodivergent leader, she is pursuing a DSW at Simmons University with a focus on Neurodivergent Leadership: Embracing Diverse Minds for Organizational Success.

www.sandrancrespo.com

www.linkedin.com/in/sandracrespo/

FINDING MY RHYTHM

JESSICA RAMIREZ, LMSW

"There is immense power in slowing down to reclaim our lives. Nothing remains static; our beginnings don't define our endings."

A LOTUS BLOOMS

I come from a long line of Guerreras—warrior women forced to disconnect from their feminine energy to fight legacies of poverty, violence, and abuse. Their strength to overcome the emotional battle scars they bore are woven into the fabric of my DNA. These familial patterns and unbroken cycles have influenced my relationships, decision making, and emotional responses, shaping the way I navigate challenges and connect with others.

For so long, I viewed these generational burdens as a curse. Now, I honor them as gifts that I traverse with the hope of healing my family. Pain travels through families until someone is ready to feel. I have consciously chosen to be that conduit. By absorbing and using the grit and resilience of my ancestors, I embrace a new culture to foster change for my son and future generations.

Born premature in the late 1970s, it was unlikely that I would survive or go on to live a full, healthy life. Yet here I am. I was born in South Carolina to teenage parents, both Colombian immigrants, who met in high school. Their unexpected pregnancy with me led to a shotgun wedding and relocation to Parris Island, SC, where my father served as a Marine. Removed from her support system, my mother struggled with isolation and postpartum depression. My father, although physically present, was ill-equipped to understand or support my mother's needs.

After my father's tour of duty, we relocated to NYC, which I believe was my parents' attempt to mend their crumbling marriage. However, emotional immaturity and external pressures took their toll. My earliest significant childhood memory is of my father leaving our home when I was three. Their divorce marked the first of several adverse childhood experiences.

Growing up in Elmhurst, Queens, I lived a colorful life, deeply influenced by a beautifully diverse immigrant community yet negatively impacted by rampant drug use in the neighborhood. With my father's departure, I came to know the complexities of life in a working, poor, single-parent household.

My mother, a survivor of complex trauma, turned to substances in a creative attempt to survive all that she was experiencing. The weight of her addiction, coupled with her intergenerational pain, left our home in a constant state of turbulence.

I witnessed my mother survive violent relationships and also experienced my own childhood sexual abuse. My abuelitos provided me refuge during my mother's darkest moments, giving me the gift of unconditional love and instilling in me faith and spirituality. Without them and my paternal titi's support, I don't know where I would be today. It really does take a village to raise a child.

On the cusp of adolescence, I supported my mother as she navigated recovery. Concerned for her well-being, I became hyper-vigilant, policing her participation in recovery meetings and monitoring the company she kept. My mother's alcoholism, my sexual abuse experience, and my father's absence affected my understanding and perception of love and security. This attachment rupture, along with my fear of abandonment, played a major role in shaping my self image and approach to intimate relationships.

When I entered high school, my mother was sober. She worked multiple jobs to put me through private school, taking great pride in providing me the educational opportunities she hadn't been afforded. I'm deeply grateful for my mother's courage in maintaining her sobriety and admire her strength as a provider. But she continued to face other challenges that made it difficult for her to offer the emotional support I needed in adolescence.

Our strained communication and what felt like her conditional love left me feeling perpetually inadequate. I developed a pattern of people-pleasing to gain her approval and avoid conflict.

Private school provided me with a firsthand understanding of positionality and privilege. While I excelled academically, I faced microaggressions from faculty. This fueled my drive for success and ignited my curiosity for community service, planting seeds for my future in social work. This period was also marked by self-discovery. I spent less time at home and more with my "homegirls," embracing all that our vibrant city had to offer in the late '90s—from hanging out on West 4th to enjoying the club scene. My friends became my sisterhood. They helped me navigate the challenges of adolescence and celebrated my coming-of-age experiences. To me, friendship is sacred, and I found my tribe—friends from similarly chaotic households, making my existence feel less isolating.

When thinking about college, I initially aspired to go away, hoping to leave my tumultuous home life behind. However, my guidance counselor discouraged me due to my financial constraints. Instead of exploring financial aid or scholarship opportunities, they urged me to stay local, and I attend St. John's University. Although I couldn't afford it there either, in typical people-pleasing fashion, I agreed.

ON A PRAYER

I began SJU with momentum, balancing a full course load as a commuter student while working full-time and embracing my inner party girl. As a first-generation college student, I had no clear direction or understanding of how to navigate higher education. Literally, all of my decisions were made on a prayer. Completely dysregulated, my undergraduate years were marked by high-risk behaviors. I sought escape and validation through overindulgence in substances, partying, and relationships without boundaries. I engaged in promiscuous behaviors, searching for the autonomy and affirmation missing in my earlier years. My lifestyle was a direct window into my internal struggles and my attempt to cope with the weight of my experiences.

During this time, I relied heavily on my childhood sister-friend also attending SJU, Jessica. She pushed me to persevere. Despite my academic challenges, I knew that dropping out wasn't an option. I didn't know how or when, but I was determined to finish my degree. I'd like to believe that my ancestors' fighting spirit guided me through this time, fueling my resolve.

As I worked on finding my rhythm, the one constant was my interest in community service. Volunteering with Mount Sinai Hospital's Sexual Assault & Violence Intervention (SAVI) Program as an emergency room advocate changed the trajectory of my life. My volunteer work, combined with my lived experiences, greatly influenced my area of study and human services career choice. After five long years, I completed my degree. For a while, I secretly believed the university had awarded me my degree in error. Struggling with imposter syndrome, I found it difficult to fully embrace my accomplishment.

After graduation, I continued working full-time in the hotel industry while searching for jobs in my field. I was constantly out, partying, and traveling with friends, using escapism to cope. While part of me was motivated to explore career opportunities, my imposter syndrome hindered me from fully embracing my potential as a bilingual candidate during the selection process. I accepted the first job offered to me, a caseworker in a foster care agency where I became overworked and underpaid. Without proper training or supervision, I couldn't provide the best support for the children and families in my caseload. I soon realized this wasn't the right fit for me. Consequently, I was proud to take on a new role as a caseworker at Elmhurst Hospital Center's (EHC) Infectious Disease Clinic in my home community of Northwest Queens. I worked with women and children infected with and affected by HIV, which allowed me to give back to my community in a meaningful way.

Around the same time, I reconnected with a childhood sweetheart. Our relationship was marked by beautiful moments of exploration, travel, and familiarity rooted in similar family backgrounds. It started as a peaceful, supportive relationship, different from the chaotic dynamics I witnessed growing up. Determined to break the generational patterns of dysfunctional intimate relationships, I was committed to nurturing what seemed like a healthy relationship.

We welcomed our son, and while motherhood brought immense joy, it also resurfaced old wounds and triggered deep-seated feelings of abandonment from my childhood. Despite my efforts to change generational patterns, my relationship eventually mirrored some of the dysfunction I had tried so hard to escape. We separated when our son turned three, and I was left grappling with the painful realization that I hadn't succeeded in breaking the family cycle. Over time, as I built a life with my son, motherhood encouraged me to reflect and hold myself accountable for change. While I'm not responsible for the generational patterns that preceded me, I am committed to disrupting those cycles going forward. In this way, being my son's mother is transformative and redemptive.

GUERRERA

In my early career, I grew increasingly dissatisfied and frustrated by the constraints of bureaucracy and leadership that didn't reflect the diverse immigrant community we served. This lack of representation impacted my ability to grow professionally. I felt powerless and stuck in the workplace. My discomfort with feeling stuck forced me to get unstuck!

With the encouragement of my mentors, I applied to graduate school after a 12-year academic hiatus and was accepted to Fordham University. Full of fear, I chose to challenge my self-defeating thoughts and embraced opportunity. Relearning how to be a student while working full-time and raising my eight-year-old son was extremely challenging. I successfully completed my first year and entered my second feeling confident and empowered.

I didn't anticipate the emotional toll social work school would have on me. For the first time in my adult life, I had to confront my trauma history. Emotionally fatigued, I realized I couldn't avoid addressing my unprocessed trauma. Inevitably, if I was going to complete my graduate program, I had to slow down and embrace my discomfort.

With the support of my therapist, I embarked on a profound healing journey. Through a trauma-informed lens, we created a safe environment where I felt secure to process my unresolved experiences. We developed techniques to alleviate the distress of my traumatic memories while engaging in inner child work to connect with my younger self and deconstruct maladaptive core beliefs. This essence of transformation marked the beginning of my lifelong commitment to healing.

Slowing down to nurture my needs supported self-regulation, giving me the traction necessary to continue my degree. I entered my third year of school with newfound confidence and a deep appreciation for the self-discovery that my studies brought me. My final field placement at a community-based mental health agency solidified my passion for clinical work. There, I provided therapy to children, teens, and adults, while clinical supervision from my field instructor deepened my understanding of the therapeutic process.

Completing graduate school was a monumental achievement. Unlike my undergraduate experience, I felt a profound sense of pride and liberation in my accomplishment. With my MSW, I no longer had to stay in an unsupportive work environment. I could now redefine my professional spaces and relationships. This milestone also demonstrated to my son the power of determination and the limitless possibilities it can create.

May this new chapter of educational achievement positively influence him and generations to come. I honor the spirit of my fierce ancestors, whose essence and legacy of perseverance inspired my path.

Shortly after graduating, a professional opportunity presented itself. A mentor reintroduced me to Mount Sinai's SAVI Program, and I joined their clinical team. This is one of my most significant professional achievements. At SAVI, I have the privilege of bearing witness to the healing journeys of immigrant survivors of gender-based violence, a population close to my heart. I draw on my own experiences to establish a safe therapeutic alliance where vulnerability is embraced and self-authenticity can be realized.

There is immense power in slowing down to reclaim our lives. Nothing remains static; our beginnings don't define our endings. Humans and our environments are constantly evolving, inviting us to surrender and adapt to change as we navigate the dance of life. As a social worker, I find my professional rhythm by embracing clinical growth with curiosity.

Personally, I continue to dance through life recognizing that my healing journey is a lifelong commitment. I embrace a holistic approach to wellness, with a strong emphasis on somatic practices. Today, yoga, prayer, and meditation are integral to my daily routine as I focus on coming home to the self and reclaiming my feminine energy. With love and gratitude, I invite you to unpack your bags and lean into the journal prompts below.

Ancestral Wisdom:

"Dios te bendiga mija, sigue adelante como el elefante."

Journal Prompts:

1. How are you dancing away from rupture and focusing on repair?

2. What steps can you take to embrace the wisdom and support of your ancestors?

3. Reflect on your favorite self—what do they look like, feel like, and embody?

BIOGRAPHY

Jessica Ramirez (she/her/ella) is a bilingual licensed master social worker and first-generation Colombian-American with over 20 years of experience in trauma-informed care. She has dedicated her career to advocating for equitable mental health resources in BIPOC communities.

Currently, Jessica is a Clinician for Mount Sinai Hospital's Sexual Assault and Violence Intervention (SAVI) program, specializing in providing holistic and integrative support to survivors of gender-based violence. Additionally, Jessica works as a Clinician with Sandoval CoLab, passionately advancing her mission to dismantle stigma related to mental health support within the Latinx/e community.

She holds a Bachelor of Arts in Sociology from St. John's University and a Master of Social Work from Fordham University. She is currently pursuing her LCSW licensure after completing post-graduate studies in integrative trauma. Her greatest life accomplishment is her son, Xavier, who continues to inspire her daily.

MICHELLE RIBADENEIRA, MSW, M.S.ED

"'For I know the plans and thoughts that I have for you,'
says the Lord, 'plans for peace and well-being and not for
disaster, to give you a future and a hope.'"
—Jeremiah 29:11 (AMP)

PLANS TO PROSPER

"Tienes la sangre dulce," is a saying used when you have a natural calling and bond with children. I hear this all the time because children always surround me. It's a simple and gratifying gift to inspire trust in a child. I think I bring that security to children and teens by being someone willing to hear them out and who they can confide in, especially in today's world, where there is so much crime and violence attacking the next generation.

From a young age, I knew I wanted to work with children and that having "sangre dulce" would have a greater purpose in my life. A purpose to prosper in a different field, going from teaching to falling into social work.

NAVIGATING A BACHELOR'S PROGRAM AS A FIRST GEN

Back in 2005, when I started at CUNY-Brooklyn College, I intended to go into Speech and Language Pathology (SLP). As I'm sure many other first-generation Americans can relate, I wasn't properly guided in college enrollment. The first cultural roadblock I had when filling out the application was answering RACE and ETHNICITY. It was a seemingly simple question, but even so, I had difficulty accepting that under RACE, I had to check off "White." Yes, my skin color was white, but the word itself made me feel like a "white girl." I am Hispanic, so under ETHNICITY, I check off Hispanic. The experience was always unsettling.

I also needed guidance in applying for financial aid, picking my classes, and getting into the SLP program. I really didn't have anyone to guide me, or at least didn't know who to ask for help. Due to the high demand, I was automatically placed on the waitlist for the SLP program, yet two years into college, I was still on the waitlist at number 64.

I distinctly remember visiting the Speech department to speak to a counselor. It felt like culture shock—everyone waiting to be seen was white. I was frustrated by how uncomfortable I felt, and even worse, after seeing a counselor who couldn't help me because of the high demand, I was told I could be on the waitlist for another year. I decided to switch to Early Childhood Special Education with a concentration in Children and Youth Studies. I loved taking the classes; I was learning not only how to become the best educator for babies with special needs, but also about advocacy, laws, casework, youth criminal justice, and sociology. I finally felt like I had a purpose in being who God wanted me to be.

It was not my own plans, but His plans, that were made to prosper, and a small mistake led me to look at my major with new eyes. I accidentally enrolled in the internship class for children and youth studies, and was placed at Brooklyn's Family Court to shadow the judge in overseeing her cases. I was excited to sit in with Ms. Elise, and learn about how to apply my academics to the real world. As ecstatic as I was about being in an internship, I soon received a notice that my financial aid was being removed because I was enrolled in a class that did not support my major. And because I was impulsive and scared that I couldn't afford college, I withdrew from the class. Ms. Elise sat me down and scolded me for withdrawing from the course before speaking with her. She explained that I could switch my concentration into a major, and that was all the encouragement I needed to declare my major in Children and Youth Studies.

PIVOTING IN MY THIRTIES

Dear Michelle Ribadeneira,

Congratulations on your admission to the Master of Social Work program at the College of Staten Island, CUNY, for the fall 2020 semester.

The letter was dated March 20, 2020. Reading the above words felt both exciting and scary. Was I crazy to go back to school at the age of 33? Furthermore… Was I crazy about getting my second master's?

Applying to the MSW program meant closing a chapter in my life and opening a new one. I graduated in 2012 with a dual bachelor's in Liberal Arts: Early Childhood/Special Education and Children and Youth Studies. At the time, I pursued my master's in Childhood Special Education as my advisor had suggested upon graduation. Once I graduated with my master's in Childhood Special Education in 2014, I told myself I would return and pursue a master's in social work when I was older. Eight years later, holding my acceptance letter to CUNY- College of Staten Island, I was doing just that.

Enrolling in college at 33 years old to purposefully switch careers, and seeing how doors opened up for me, was just another sign from God that this was the path I needed to take. I had mere weeks to get three professional reference letters, all my medical records, my college transcript, a Purpose Statement, and my application handed in. I also realized I needed to take Statistics 101 before applying. Just thinking about the process brings me chills and tears. I ended up reaching out to Ms. Elise Goldberg, the program director at Brooklyn College's Youth and Children's Studies, hoping she would remember me eight years later. She did, and helped me with my recommendation letter and personal statement essay.

Everything was going well; I handed in all the paperwork, I was on track to pass the Statistics class, and I was still working full-time teaching Bilingual Spanish world first grade. Suddenly, COVID-19 hit, putting a pause on in-person teaching. Learning statistics and probability through Zoom was different, but I was thankful for the professor's creativity and understanding. During that time, not being able to go outside because of the pandemic made my anxiety skyrocket, and I relied on interacting with others through technology.

In the end, the hard work—all those stressful moments of checking my email constantly, the migraines from being on the computer for hours, the scramble for paperwork, making sure I supplied enough work for my students, ensuring to stayed connected with friends—all paid off with the letter of acceptance in my hand. A letter I knew would change my life for the better, a letter that brought challenges and isolation but also brought me closer to trusting God with the process. That letter meant growth and new beginnings.

FINDING COMMUNITY AS EVERYTHING SHIFTED

My family means the world to me; through them, I know the meaning of community, love, and respect. We have always been tight-knit, and I still travel to Ecuador every summer. I want to say that it's because of my trips to Ecuador that I was raised with empathy for others. In Ecuador, I saw poverty firsthand—children living in the streets, begging for money or selling candy. My grandparents and parents always helped others, especially family and friends, whether with a plate of food, spare clothes, or a place to stay. The love of God was always seen through their actions, ones I learned to carry on as I grew older.

However, throughout my academic journey, finding community and acceptance in school was hard for me. Growing up, my dad placed me in a private catholic school in Brooklyn, NY. In Ecuador, it is thought that private schools provide the best education. I recognize my dad worked hard to afford my tuition, but it wasn't an ideal experience. The Catholic school was predominantly white and wealthy, and I was not accepted by my teachers. According to them, my homework was so neat, they assumed my parents did it for me. On other days, I was not smart enough to do the work because it was completely wrong. I would shut down and internalize these comments. I felt immense imposter syndrome—but for Latinas like myself, how can I even call it imposter syndrome, when I was actually being told I wasn't good enough?

I needed a safe place to escape problems going on at home, but school was never the refuge I sought. I didn't fit in with the other kids, and would have friends for a few months only to be discarded by the end of the year. The adults who were supposed to advocate, help, and accept me did not. Once I got to 8th grade, I told my parents I wanted to go to public school.

College of Staten Island is where I finally found a school community. My experience in the MSW program during the pandemic is where I realized how much I appreciated being accepted. I was able to share that I was a Christian, actively involved at church. I was not ashamed of being who I was—33, single, religious, and looking for a new career. I did not have professors who told me I was not smart enough or ignored me, and I made friendships over Zoom with students from different races, ethnicities, ages, and various abilities. Coming together for the wellbeing of our own mental health was a relief; we supported and checked in on each other throughout the year.

My professor, Dr. Archibald, always started the class by asking us what we did that week for our mental health. Our homework was to make sure we set aside time for our mental health and not become burnt out by work, school, and internships. I had professors who took us into their homes, sharing space with their pets, and I met students who would openly share their struggles and understandings. While navigating our own mental health, we completed internships and served clients. And as the world shifted, we built community.

In this way, while the pandemic was a season of shifting, it was also one of community.

FINDING MY VOICE AND TRUSTING THE FUTURE

Everything had a purpose. I found my voice in the middle of the COVID-19 pandemic—a voice to advocate for myself and those around me. For many years, I was always criticized for not having a "teacher's voice" in the classroom. Yet in my master's program, my professor Patti Gross, alongside my classmates, explained that my voice is very soothing, and because of it, she could see why my clients felt safe around me, no matter their age. The voice that was always criticized because it was not appropriate for classroom management became the voice that was loud and clear to advocate for what others may need.

"Tienes la sangre dulce" had a new meaning for this path I was embarking on. Because of my sweetness, students and their families come to me with trust and openness. Even middle schoolers and teenagers are comfortable being themselves around me, when we know how difficult it is for adolescents to open up. Because of my experience when I was young, what I saw growing up, and even my own experience of troubles at home, I try my best to be secure and help families find a place where they can trust me to help them.

I am thankful to my very first mentors, my parents, professors, and school staff who helped undo the harm I experienced in my early school years. I see how bold they were. I see the fire in their heart. I hear them roar and see them not just survive, but thrive as Latinas. My heart is filled with gratitude that I am now a mentor to many, and I recognize my power in this role.

I love working in the school system because I can do so much more for families there. School should be a safe place for students, especially if they're going through things at home. I also know that God has a plan on purpose, and wherever He takes me next will have the same impact. I can only trust whatever He has in store for me, and I know I will always say yes to helping those around me.

A special thank you to Dr. Edith Chaparro for sponsoring and mentoring me.

Ancestral Wisdom:

My abuelita gave me bendiciones from afar. Las bendiciones always worked and helped me believe I was protected and loved. Blessings are also called affirmations and prayers. Making sure you say them to yourself can support your mental health.

Journal Prompts:
1. Was there a time when you felt you were not enough? How did you overcome that negative thought?
2. What does community mean to you and what does your community look like?
3. What would you tell your younger self? Close your eyes and speak to them.

BIOGRAPHY

Michelle Ribadeneira, an Ecuadorian American, recently completed her Master's in Social Work and is working towards her LMSW. She earned a Master's in Special Education in 2014 and now serves as a school-based counselor at Greater Brunswick Charter School (GBCS) in New Jersey.

At GBCS, she developed bilingual mental health workshops and launched the first Mental Health Assembly. Outside work, Michelle leads youth and dance ministries at Harvest Community Church and runs a small business, Mishi's Delights. She also hosts the podcast Cafecito and Real Talk and co-authored Today's Young Inspired Latina Vol. V. Michelle is committed to promoting mental health and empowering her community.

Instagram accounts:
Mishi_alexandra
Mishisdelights
Cafecito_and_realtalk
LinkedIn: www.linkedin.com/in/michelle-ribadeneira-msw

STEPHANIE SORADY, LCSW

"It is important for all of us to appreciate where we come from and how that history has really shaped us in ways that we might not understand." —Sonia Sotomayor

MULTICULTURAL BEGINNING

My parents met while working at a Taco Bell in Los Angeles. My dad was a third-generation Irish/Hungarian American, and my mom had recently immigrated to the United States from Mexico in hopes of a future filled with opportunities. He was a hard-working blue-collar New Yorker, and she was the life of the party with an infectious smile. They were young, in love, and expecting a baby sooner than their Catholic parents would've liked. I was that baby. Many friends and family members on both sides doubted the relationship. They came from different countries, languages, cultural expectations, and ethnicities. Could two people from such different backgrounds make it work?

As the firstborn daughter, I became a key player in ensuring things worked between them. For many years, it was just the three of us. I helped translate not only linguistic but also cultural barriers that arose between them. My parents have joked that I was their "therapist" long before I even knew what a therapist was. After a fight, I'd often go back and forth between my parents, trying to help them understand each other's perspective and encouraging them to use "I" statements in the future.

My dad is the hardest-working person I've ever met, but because he worked at a bar, he was often gone on nights and weekends. As a result, I became my mother's partner in his absence. I was her shoulder to cry on, I was who she turned to for advice, and I was the first person she would excitedly share ideas and plans with. She needed me; I didn't know another way of being. I spoke English more fluently, I was a citizen, and I had white-passing privileges while she experienced discrimination.

I was often the only witness to the constant microaggressions she faced as an immigrant and woman of color. I remember my mom taking me shopping for clothes, only to be openly followed by a boutique employee the entire time. I can't even recall how often my mom was mistakenly assumed to be a nanny at the park or school functions. In return for the emotional support I gave her, my mom taught me to fill any situation with joy and gratitude, from singing Luis Miguel songs while we cleaned our apartment to making every meal a delicious event.

From a young age, my parents' needs became my own. Boundaries were non-existent. In many ways, our parent-child roles had reversed. That isn't to say they didn't give me love or work incredibly hard to provide me with everything they could. There were more significant systemic and intergenerational issues at play, which ultimately led to me being the primary emotional caregiver stepping in to help with logistical tasks as needed, like navigating a flawed healthcare system. It would take me decades to realize that my experiences had a name—parentification.

When I was twelve, my little brother Thomas was born, followed by my baby sister Sophia between my quinceanera and sweet sixteen. Instantly, I loved them with all my heart and knew I'd do anything for them. Yet the birth of my siblings also officially solidified my development of "eldest daughter syndrome." Like parentification, this term encapsulates the all-too-common phenomenon in which the eldest-born daughter takes on disproportionate responsibilities within the family. Essentially, eldest daughters become the third parent even if they are still kids. Both parentification and eldest-daughter syndrome are patterns we often see in many Latine and immigrant families. I am sure many of you reading this understand exactly what I'm describing.

A few months after Sophia was born, my dad came home from work late one night and woke me from my spot on the couch. He was taking over my shift of watching the baby. As I groggily got up to drag myself to bed, aware I had school in the morning, he placed a hand on my forearm to stop me. "These are your babies, too," he said. "If anything happens to your mom and me, you've got to take care of them. Make sure you all stay together." My heart started to thump at the idea of being a 15-year-old responsible for two little ones. I wanted to tell him I was scared. I wanted to tell him I was tired and this was hard enough. But instead, I did what any "good" daughter would do. I nodded and said, "Of course, Dad, I promise."

WHO IS THE PARENT?

Parentification can disguise itself as a kid being "responsible" or "mature for their age." But in reality, parentification occurs as a survival response. Parentification involves a kid taking on tasks and responsibilities that aren't developmentally appropriate. For example, mediating adults' conflicts, being in charge of younger siblings getting to school, or worrying about paying the bills. Parentified kids do tasks that are not age-appropriate to help keep the family system going. The reason we see this occurring in many Latine and immigrant families is that the United States doesn't have systems in place to support the health and well-being of these communities. On the contrary, our communities are frequently marginalized in every sense of the word.

Additionally, parentification tends to happen when there is untreated substance use disorder, severe mental illness, or the effects of incarceration in the home. As we social workers know all too well, appropriate resources, education, and systemic change could help mitigate these stressors. If that were the case, more kids would be allowed to be kids. The consequences of parentification can be loss of childhood experiences, anxiety, and overwhelm. Long-term, this may look like codependency, relationship difficulties, low self-esteem, and a negative impact on mental well-being.

I'm speaking about parentification from both personal and professional experience. From military veterans to college students, I've had the honor of serving different community members in my career. Almost as if by magic, I also tend to attract a lot of adults who were parentified as kids. Many of them are in helping professions as well! Parentification is more common than we think, and is an aspect of our society that requires more awareness and attention.

Moreover, when assessing eldest-daughter syndrome, it's evident that sex and gender also play a role in who bears the brunt of responsibilities. While this is certainly not always the case, many families have cultural expectations that girls should be the caretakers while boys can just be… boys. We also see this reflected in Latine culture through marianismo and machismo. Too many daughters are expected to help raise younger siblings, do household chores, manage other people's emotions, and disregard their needs. It wasn't until I was in my MSW program, sitting with my therapist, that I had an epiphany: I had already been social working for most of my life.

Ironically, this epiphany left me with a lot of questions. Did I love the work, or was I just reasonably good at it because of my upbringing? Did I have a savior complex? What career path would I have chosen if things at home had been different? Was it possible to heal from the distress of parentification? Then, the age-old refrain—was there something wrong with me? It's interesting how, as humans, we tend to think that our flaws and scars are the unique things about us. When we're in the depths of self-doubt, it can be challenging to recognize that you are not alone.

Many of us are drawn to social work because it feels familiar. The skills required to be a social worker, such as communication, advocacy, assessing resources, and emotional intelligence, are nearly second nature to us. Several incredible social workers I've met also have first-hand experience with parentification. This shows us that parentification doesn't only create adverse side effects—it also nourishes community healing. For many Latines, caring for family and community is integral to our culture. We often laugh, celebrate, struggle, grieve, and live in communal environments. This desire to look out for each other is one of the aspects of my culture I love the most. Eso, ¡y nuestro sazón en la cocina!

PRIORITIZING HEALING

Attending therapy was vital in recognizing the advantages and disadvantages of growing up parentified. Therapy is also the best investment I've ever made in my social work career. I could see how creative I was, a must for social work, because I had been problem-solving for my family since childhood. On the other hand, I noticed that this also led to me having a "rescue impulse." It took a lot of practice, but I could now acknowledge the rescue impulse popping up when working with clients. I was able to contain the feeling and focus on empowering them instead. This healing journey also prompted me to develop intentional boundaries for the first time. Boundaries helped me be less resentful in my relationships and mitigate burnout at work. It's not easy, but I'm still working at it. The best part? My therapist is also a Latina with a mixed background, and I was able to do this work while integrating my culture.

As we've seen, adults who experienced parentification in childhood and subsequently entered the social work field often grapple with unique challenges that can impact their well-being and professional effectiveness. The demanding nature of social work, coupled with the emotional residue of early parentification, can contribute to burnout, compassion fatigue, and vicarious trauma. Prioritizing self-care and engaging in a healing process is not merely a personal indulgence but an ethical imperative for us. By addressing our unmet needs and unresolved trauma, we can cultivate greater emotional resilience, enhance our capacity for empathy, and ultimately provide more effective and sustainable care for our clients.

Thank you to my Madrina, Jacqueline Aviles-Torres, for her sponsorship and mentorship during this narrative journey.

Ancestral Wisdom:

A la mejor cocinera se le queman los frijoles. (The best cook gets burnt beans.) Give yourself and others grace. We are not perfect.

Journal Prompts:

1. How did your family background influence your decision to pursue a career in social work?
2. What qualities do you possess that can act as both strengths and weaknesses?
3. How can you continue to invest in your healing?

BIOGRAPHY

Stephanie Sorady is a licensed clinical social worker, author, and field instructor at California State University, Los Angeles. As the proud daughter of a Mexican immigrant, Stephanie's passion for removing the stigma around mental health is fueled by her personal and professional experiences. She has penned a bilingual self-love poetry collection, *Kiss From God*, and *The Better Habits Workbook*, both aimed at helping individuals heal and achieve their goals. Stephanie is the owner of Luz Trauma Therapy, a private practice that specializes in healing from parentification and trauma. She resides in her hometown of Los Angeles, California.

Website: www.luztraumatherapy.com
Instagram: https://www.instagram.com/stephaniesorady/
The Better Habits Workbook: https://shorturl.at/evEPZ
Kiss from God: https://shorturl.at/knpqH

Sources:

- Cole, T. (2021, August 09). Navigating parentification: Understanding and healing the role reversal in parent-child relationships [Audio podcast episode].
- Dariotis, J. K., Chen, F. R., Park, Y. R., Nowak, M. K., French, K. M., & Codamon, A. M. (2023). Parentification Vulnerability, Reactivity, Resilience, and Thriving: A Mixed Methods Systematic Literature

Review. *International journal of environmental research and public health*, 20(13), 6197. https://doi.org/10.3390/ijerph20136197

- Hamilton, A. (2021, August 09). Parentification: Signs and Symptoms of a Parentified Child. Embark Behavioral Health. Retrieved from https://embarkbh.com/parenting/parentification-signs-and-symptoms-of-a-parentified-child/

RAFAEL TEJADA, LCSW

"As our ability to know and heal ourselves deepens, we will be better equipped to examine the world more carefully and heal it more effectively." —**Yung Pueblo**

PART I: THE DARKNESS

How long have I been disconnected from myself? Is that the question? Or is it, *why have I felt so disconnected from myself?* Was I even aware of the level of disconnection?

These are some of the questions I considered when I began to experience more embodiment. It didn't happen all at once. I didn't wake up one day suddenly feeling connected with mind, body, and soul. No, quite the contrary… it was a much slower process, at times painful and difficult to tolerate. It was more like waking up every day knowing something wasn't right. There was a tendency to be pulled in the direction where that discomfort would find some form of relief, ignoring the faint echo traveling through the darkness of a space I dared not explore and, instead, choosing to alleviate that discomfort with distractions of the mind. It was a robotic existence where the mind is safest in the familiarity of daily routines; the world showed me what to do, where to go, how to do it—so I did it. Ignoring that distant echo. Fearing what it could say to me, or worse, fearing what it might ask of me. At times not even hearing it at all.

Becoming a father changed my relationship with myself. I had just finished my third semester of the Master of Social Work program and was about to embark on a journey through truly unchartered waters. So, naturally I did what came easiest to me—I allowed my brain (not my body) to lead me and consulted with others on what I should feel. I was told how I would feel when I first held my son. I was told that the connection would be immediate and undeniable.

What nobody told me was how hard it would be to connect with your newborn son while being disconnected from yourself. My desire to connect with my son was deep; I witnessed the beauty of his life coming into this world. I welcomed him, nervous and afraid. Trying to focus on what I thought I should be feeling and ignoring everything my body was telling me, I chose not to hear the call to embrace the full range of emotions

I experienced that day. I was looking for happiness alone. My connection with him was limited by my own inability to feel connected to all parts of myself. Feeling like I failed at something so significant, I felt unworthy.

What I didn't realize at the time was how I came to feel so disconnected, ignoring the more complex and difficult parts of me. Why did I push away my own intuition and emotions? Why did I avoid facing the darkness?

MI BELLA FAMILIA

I could never attempt to understand myself, especially the disconnection I felt, without considering my origins. The story of my ancestors is my story as well. I come from a truly beautiful family, imperfect in all the ways that make them human. Their wisdom gets passed down, and sometimes it comes in the form of old pain—in effect, old wounds. Often, it's the kind of pain you can't see. Pain that stems from survival.

My father came to New York City from "el campo." He was 17 years old when it was decided that he would travel to NY in search of a brighter future. Growing up, I knew little about my father's life in the Dominican Republic; I knew that he had a fifth grade education and a father he rarely spoke about. I knew that my grandmother was grumpy and rigid, at least with me. I have many memories of being scolded by her because I struggled to sit still. I also knew that my father came here and worked his butt off to get ahead and provide for his family. He had an entrepreneurial mind and used it to his advantage.

I've learned many lessons from the successes of my father, but what has stuck with me the most has been watching my dad pick himself back up after every failure. He has never given up, never complained, and never taken no for an answer. Similarly, I have learned so much from my mother, who has always been hardworking as well as kind and compassionate. She is selfless in too many ways to note here, almost to a fault, something she learned from her father.

The thing about learning from our parents as children is that we don't get to pick and choose what we take away and what we would like to leave behind. We also learn from the ways they've learned to survive in this world. Along with my dad's impressive work ethic came an abandonment of self and lack of self-awareness. His is an ego manipulated by a patriarchal framework that limited his openness to acknowledging the full range of his own emotions. So, when my father wanted to pass down lessons forged by these beliefs, he could not consider that they would impact how I connected with myself.

My father once told me, "El dia que tengas más hambre, ponte un palillo en la boca y haste como si acabas de comer." I always admired my dad's pride, but I'll never forget this lesson because it helped me see how I was taught to shut down important parts of myself. How so early in life I learned to ignore my own gut and intuition, and how I was taught that ignoring my needs would help me survive in a world that was harsh and many times unfair. My father wasn't wrong; this was the world he lived in and the way he learned to survive in it. Emotional awareness did not hold high enough value in his reality, so his body and brain justified these ways of surviving.

My mother, in her own selfless ways, did the impossible so my sister and I felt joy and safety. She made sure that basic needs were never an issue, even during the hardest times. My mother was so good at this that we barely noticed my father's bankruptcy while losing our childhood home. The price for this was blatantly ignoring some very difficult and dark emotions for herself, as well as not allowing my sister and I to understand what we were feeling. It's not like I didn't notice difficult times—it's that I felt I couldn't ask about them and explore what was obvious to me.

I learned to look away and avoid the big and uncomfortable emotions. This was about survival.

BACK IN MY BODY

What does healing mean to me? Healing is something that can happen every day of our lives. It's usually happening in the moments we least expect it.

When I began my traditional educational journey, I had no idea which direction I was heading in. All I knew was that I had curiosities that needed to be explored; something was telling me that the universe had more in store for me. For a long time, I shied away from formal education, mainly because I held a deeply ingrained belief that I was not good at school. Life had taught me that I was quite good at learning from real world experiences, but my childhood had caused a deep insecurity with formal education. I didn't understand why I felt so inadequate, because

I felt that I was bright. I noticed how I could learn certain things with ease, at times grasping challenging concepts before my peers and then explaining it to them.

I have clear memories of feeling like I was good at some things but struggling with everything else. This became very apparent from about fifth grade on. During these years I slowly shut down, like a flame flickering and gradually losing its strength and brightness. I began seeing myself more and more like the narrative painted by teachers: "He talks too much in class... He keeps turning around to speak to his friends... He doesn't listen... He never finishes his work... He needs to try harder." It became easier to believe that I just wasn't cutting it. I was one of the bad kids—detention became a familiar place, and my friend group began to change.

I didn't know what was wrong or how to ask for help, and neither did my parents. Coming from a hard-working immigrant family meant your only option was to figure it out. They knew nothing else other than hard work and personal sacrifice. Being born in New York was a tremendous privilege, so I had no excuse. What they understood was that I wasn't trying hard enough, and in part they weren't wrong. However, I hadn't yet figured out what was getting in the way.

At 17 years old, already a year behind all my friends and classmates, I decided to drop out of school mainly because it no longer made sense to continue trying to accomplish something I couldn't envision. My insecurities with education had gotten the best of me, and I was convinced there was no point to another year in high school. I'll never forget the sadness in my mother's eyes. I promised her that I would get my GED and convinced her to sign me out of school. She pleaded with a school guidance counselor to help change my mind. He was cold and disinterested, telling her, "Your son has already made up his mind." This further validated my feeling that I didn't belong there.

That same week I registered for a GED course and shortly after that I passed the exam on my first try. I even attended the GED citywide graduation. There was my mom, always supporting me. Always proud. A very kind lady at the GED program said I might have what it takes for college and that I should give it a try. She helped me with the City University of New York application, and I registered at Kingsborough Community College for the following semester. A, B, and C were my first semester grades for mostly remedial courses. I dropped out my second semester. I couldn't pinpoint why; I felt disengaged and unsure what I was doing there.

Soon after I casually bumped into a high school friend at the neighborhood gym who had just started working as an Emergency Medical Technician. My curiosity sparked again. A few days later I was enrolled at the John Jay EMT-Basic program, and soon enough I was working as an EMT.

Yet somehow this still wasn't enough. I felt like I could do more. I met some paramedics at work and became curious about their jobs and salaries. I talked my way into the next paramedic class despite not having the one year of experience they required. I had a rude awakening when classes began. I failed my first exam and experienced a rush of very familiar emotions and insecurities, feeling like I wasn't cut out for the academic part of this work. However, this time around I noticed something about the way I learned in groups. So, I began to host study groups at my place before exams. It turns out that I grasped the material so much better when I could discuss and help teach it to others. I felt I finally figured out what had been getting in the way throughout my educational career. My confidence grew and I successfully passed the program and the licensing exam.

Being a paramedic was fun, but it wasn't long before I began to feel the itch for more. Growing uneasy always caused me to try multiple things at once, and this time I explored my interest in business. I spent the next few years trying different business ventures, one idea after another. Very few would materialize and others would fade out. Ultimately, I felt lost, seeking meaning in a career but struggling to believe in myself.

In 2010, I made one of the most important decisions of my life when I decided to give school another try and registered at LaGuardia Community College. What made this decision significant wasn't that I decided to attend college, but the fact that for the first time in a long time I listened to my intuition. I listened to that faint voice telling me that I am worthy and capable of more. It begged for my attention and encouraged me to tend to very deep needs of being heard and seen. I didn't know it at the time, but looking back now, I knew deep down what I had to do. It was the most connected to myself that I'd been in years, and it only got better from there. I allowed myself to make decisions based on my curiosities, which felt like a huge privilege that at times I felt guilty about. Allowing myself to be curious and following my intuition is what led me to become a social worker and psychotherapist. But this realization wouldn't come until later in my journey.

There came a time when I had to face myself and all parts of me, when I had to hold myself accountable and truly assess my own awareness and capacity. It was a time when the lessons, books, and tools I accumulated throughout my life were not enough. This was also a time when I needed to meet myself like I hadn't done before. For me, this was when I realized what taking care of oneself really looked like, and that listening to my intuition would be how I'd thrive. I realized that embodiment means knowing myself fully, and that my deep desire to help others heal requires self-compassion and self-acceptance. Through my own healing, this is also the way that I'll be the father that my son needs.

Thank you to my parents and family for helping mold the person I am today, and thank you to my madrina of social work, Camila Pastor, who has guided, taught, and believed in me during my healing and professional journey.

Ancestral Wisdom:

In the words of my dad, the comeback kid: "Never give up, keep going."

Journal Prompts:

1. In what ways do you feel disembodied or disconnected from yourself?
2. Think about the parts of yourself that you may not trust. What prevents you from trusting them?
3. What lessons can you learn from exploring your family history or ancestry?

BIOGRAPHY

Born and raised in Brooklyn, NY, Rafael Tejada is the proud son of Dominican immigrants. After starting a career as an EMS paramedic, Rafael earned a Bachelor's in Liberal Arts and Master's in Child Development from Sarah Lawrence College. He then received a Master's of Social Work from New York University. Rafael currently works as a Clinical Supervisor & Psychotherapist for NYC Health + Hospitals.

He sees the culmination of his life's diverse experiences and education in his role as a psychotherapist. His journey is a testament to resilience, determination, and the relentless pursuit of one's dreams, and he has a deep-rooted commitment to helping others achieve theirs.

Our Leaves:
Complexity, Legacy, and the Beauty of Transformation

———

LESSONS OF RESILIENCE FROM MIS PADRES AND MIS ABUELOS

LAUDY BURGOS, LCSW-R, PMH-C

"My grandmother's eyes told me to be strong and reminded me that I came from a long line of strong, proud ancestors."

MIS PADRES Y MIS ABUELOS

My childhood was filled with good memories my parents worked hard to create. The daughter of Costa Rican immigrants, I was surrounded by love, laughter, trust, and joy, and my parents provided a home where there was unity and lots of supportive advice. As I grew older and needed to start figuring some things out myself, my parents always knew the perfect balance of when to intervene and when to allow me to make mistakes that I would eventually learn from. They gave me the tools I needed not only to survive painful moments, but also to help me move on and thrive. It was during my divorce and through experiencing motherhood that I used those tools to cope and heal.

My paternal grandmother, Tita Landy, was born in a small town in Costa Rica. Despite only having a sixth-grade education, she was smart, ambitious, and curious about the world. She married as a teenager and had six children. While she loved her family, she was a victim of intimate partner violence, silently enduring years of suffering as a housewife because she didn't want her children to struggle.

One day she saw a newspaper advertisement recruiting women to work in America as nannies/housekeepers. To her, it wasn't only an opportunity to leave an abusive marriage; it was also an opportunity for her children. Those first months on Long Island were rough—she scrubbed floors on her knees and went to bed exhausted. I can't imagine what it must have been like to leave her country, her home, and her children to come to a strange place where she couldn't always communicate and wasn't always welcome.

Within a year she had an apartment in West Harlem (the same building where I still live) and green cards for her three younger children, as well as my father. Despite never learning English, she managed to enroll her children in school and help family and friends with anything they needed for years to come. My tita always knew what to say to make me feel better and gave her love and wise advice in abundance. She was a critical thinker who always had the solution to our problems and a trusted confidante who protected us fiercely. She was the pillar and rock of our family. She taught me that suffering is part of life but emphasized that suffering builds endurance, which builds character and eventually hope. She saw my success before I did and spoke it into existence, because that's what Latina grandmothers do!

My maternal grandfather, Tito Manuel, immigrated here as an adult, but he too found his way. We gathered in his small apartment in Queens where he joked with his grandchildren, told stories, and was always the life of the party. He was the glue that held us together. Despite losing two young daughters, he embraced life and taught me the value of finding joy, even in the depths of heartache.

THE DIVORCE

I met my first husband in college and married him right after graduate school. A year later, our son Jonathan was born. We quickly became a family and cherished our moments with him. But 18 months later, September 11 happened, and my police officer husband experienced trauma and saw things no human should ever see. He lost friends and cleaned up debris and human remains. Hearing his stories and seeing how he went from a happy and jovial person to someone more somber and reserved vicariously traumatized me. But Jonathan made our lives so beautiful amid all the uncertainty, so we decided to embrace life, and I became pregnant with Brianna.

During that pregnancy, things began to change in our marriage, and my husband left. I was stunned and felt like the rug had been pulled out from under me. I was left feeling abandoned, betrayed, and alone. At 27, I was now a single mother to two beautiful children who would need me more than ever.

At first, the divorce was incredibly painful, and I'm grateful that my family lived in the same building and provided unwavering support. My father gave loving but firm advice, sugar-coating nothing and laying everything out in realistic terms because he wanted me to get through this heartache with dignity and strength. He lent me money to purchase my first car, with a reminder that I didn't need to depend on anyone and could still do everything I did before the divorce. It felt like he was pushing me too quickly, but I later realized it was his way of helping me move forward and do what I needed to do for myself and my children.

My mother and sisters helped me with childcare and daily support. My sisters shared meals with me and spent time with me on weekends so I wouldn't feel lonely. Although my mom and I didn't talk much about what happened, she told me stories that lifted my spirits, like anecdotes from her childhood and the amazing things my children did every day with her. Some nights we would go to Target, laughing and gossiping while we shopped.

My grandmother had suffered a stroke and couldn't speak. I saw the pain in her eyes, but they also spoke louder than any words—her eyes told me to be strong and reminded me that I came from a long line of resilient, proud ancestors.

WHEN IT RAINS, IT POURS

During the divorce, I found out Jonathan had a speech delay and needed early intervention services. I remember how complex the system was and how they wanted to label my son as having autism because he was a brown boy, and not because they had necessarily done all the appropriate testing. I told them that a lot of what they were seeing was Jonathan's emotional reaction to the divorce. I also reminded them that I was a social worker who had worked with infants and toddlers and had a few ideas about what could be wrong with my child. But they insisted that he would never be in a regular school and that I had to accept their diagnosis.

My mother told me that Jonathan just needed some time and that my instincts would tell me what I needed to do. My dad reminded me that no matter what, Jonathan was still the affectionate, happy child he'd always been. My parents empowered me to push back and question the system, and I'm glad I did because while Jonathan was eventually diagnosed with ADHD, he did not have autism. I spent two hours at a meeting advocating for my son to receive center-based services at a school of my choice, where he thrived; he was later mainstreamed into a regular school. Now, he's a successful electrical engineer.

After Brianna's birth, I experienced postpartum depression, but I pushed through the same way my parents did. Even when they experienced hardship, their goal was always to get us to the finish line as successful adults. I started therapy and thought about how far my family had come. How my dad struggled with

English when he immigrated, yet he learned the language, was an honors student, and worked hard. How difficult it must have been for my undocumented mother to work in a factory, dreading when immigration services might come and detain her. How scary it was to navigate the healthcare and educational systems even after she got her green card. All these things propelled me forward.

A NEW BEGINNING

Almost four years after my divorce, I met a wonderful man who came into my and my children's life at the perfect time. Despite my happiness, I found it difficult to trust, still holding on to some resentment from my failed first marriage. Once again, my dad provided clarity and reminded me how important stability is to children, something he had modeled for me. I also thought about my parents' relationship—they'll celebrate their fiftieth anniversary this year—and how all their interactions were lessons. They didn't need Valentine's Day to celebrate their love; they celebrated their love all the time. They did things to please each other, even when it was uncomfortable. They never cursed at each other, and on hard days they gave each other extra grace.

My mother—a chronic overthinker and worrier—taught me the value of not stressing over things that won't matter in a few days or months. She always spoke about how peaceful and happy one of her aunts was at the end of her life because she didn't let things fester. I'm now allowing myself that grace so I can cope when things are rough. In particular, I'm letting go of the past and forgiving, something my mom taught me is a gift to yourself more than to the other person. It has been freeing, and when apologies come, they're more meaningful.

After two years of dating, I married my current husband—a divorcé with children too—and a year later we had our daughter Gabrielle, who completed our family. As a family we've traveled to different places and relied on each other for support. It also helps that we lived in the same building as my parents, and they were just an elevator ride away. One of the best things about our Latino culture is the community that surrounds us, ready to step in to help.

THE SEASONS OF LIFE

As life goes on, we experience heartbreak, illness, hope, opportunity, growth, failure, achievement. It's critical to reflect on the lessons these seasons bring. When we are younger, there's a strong need to be right, but to stay in a relationship with someone, you must compromise, be willing to lose some battles, and let go of your ego. This was another big lesson my parents taught me: humility is key.

As my children grew, I felt a deep sadness that somehow I was losing them. I realized this was how my parents felt when I was trying to find my way and discover who I was. So I've adapted to the changing relationships with Jonathan and Brianna and was delighted to see that the distance didn't take away from the depth of our relationship. I've had some of the most meaningful conversations with them in the past few years.

There was also a season of loss—my grandparents' deaths weren't easy. I still miss them, and sometimes I worry that as time passes, I'll forget our memories. Yet there are moments when their presence is strong, and it brings a smile to my face. It can be something simple, like how I cook a certain dish, or something more meaningful, like when I remember a conversation we had. They continue to live on through my parents and me.

My work life has been extremely satisfying, but not without painful moments. Success and promotions have come at a cost. When you're a Latina and you move up, there are parts of your identity that you lose. As I grow older, I'm trying to hold onto all those parts of my identity for dear life! It's a fine balance between asserting yourself when necessary and knowing when to remain quiet. I'm learning to "sit still" as my mentor, Judy, always taught me.

There are seasons when my faith is tested, and I realize motherhood's difficulties. Sometimes I feel like I've failed as a parent. Over the last year, I've leaned on my parents to nurture me and remind me that no parent is perfect, and we must trust the foundation we give our children. They've also taught me to set boundaries with compassion, and to be patient even on days when I feel like giving up. Yet the most important lesson has been that these seasons pass and that God will see you through it.

I'm so grateful to have parents who know exactly what to say when I most need it. I hope that I can do the same for my children and that one day they think that I'm at least half as good as my parents have been to me.

Ancestral Wisdom

My mom always says, *"No hay mal que dure cien años ni cuerpo que lo aguante."*

Journal Prompts

1. What are the lessons that have been passed down to you that build your resilience?

2. When experiencing challenges, what mental health and/or holistic support do you seek?

3. What are the biggest lessons you have learned from your family/ancestors?

BIOGRAPHY

Laudy Burgos, LCSW-R, PMH-C is a bilingual English/Spanish licensed clinical social worker with over 26 years of experience in the areas of perinatal mood disorders and family and children's services. Burgos is trained in trauma-informed treatment approaches including Eye Movement Desensitization and Reprocessing (EMDR) and Interpersonal Therapy (IPT).

She is currently the Associate Director at Mount Sinai Hospital in the Department of Social Work Services. Burgos received her Bachelor's of Science and Master's in Social Work from NYU Silver School of Social Work. Burgos is an adjunct faculty member in the BSW program at NYU and the MSW program at Columbia University. She is also a board member at Postpartum Support International and Siembra Today.

NAVIGATING THE PATH OF MENTORSHIP

DR. EDITH CHAPARRO, PHD, LCSW-R

"My vision is to create hope and teach you to trust your process no matter what twists and turns might occur. Learning is not linear; your path will lead you to where you are meant to be."

HEARTFELT INSPIRATIONS

I was born and raised in New York as a first-generation American. My parents immigrated from South America— Paraguay—in the 1960s. They were in their early twenties when they left behind their parents, siblings, home, and friends to seek opportunities, as their country was under a dictatorship. I reflect on the sacrifices my parents made so that I could have freedom and success that would have been impossible if they had remained in Paraguay. My parents were the only members of their families who immigrated to the United States, so we have no other family here—holidays and special occasions were spent with my parents and a few close friends. As a child, I often thought about what it would be like to go to grandma's house for the weekend or a cousin's wedding or birthday party. Growing up without relatives made me feel isolated, with a lack of familial support and connection. I journaled almost daily, which helped with healing that sense of loneliness. Moreover, my mother's support helped me develop a sense of independence and self-resilience.

For as long as I can remember, I spent summer school break in Paraguay. We stayed at my maternal grandmother's house in a small town called Barrio Jara, Asunción, where all the neighbors knew each other and everyone's business. When I arrived with my mother, I recall neighbors and relatives coming by to say hello and bring typical Paraguayan cookies called chipitas. They would stare at my clothes, look me up and down, and comment on my appearance, saying things like, "Estás gorda" (You look fat) or "Can I have your sneakers when you leave?" I felt angry and insulted; I also lacked fluency in Spanish, so I felt stuck with words. Luckily, my grandmother, mi abuelita, shooed them away and kicked them out of her home.

During my time in Paraguay, I established a close

relationship with my *abuelita;* I admired her strength, humor, and selfless personality. My mother has similar characteristics, and I am confident I have inherited these traits as well. My grandmother was a seamstress; along with being creative, she had excellent business skills and a no-nonsense attitude. I respected my grandmother immensely; in Latino culture, *respeto* is an essential value where we show high regard for older family members through dignity and understanding. Learning about cultural beliefs helped me be proud of my heritage and enhanced my self-awareness, as well as my personal growth.

Abuelita inspired me through her valuable wisdom and insights. I admired her determination as she raised three children, including my mother, as a single mother. Sadly, her oldest daughter, Beba, suddenly passed away, and she was faced with raising her toddler-aged granddaughter while grieving. My aunt Beba's death was the first loss I encountered; I was around eight years old, and I witnessed my mother suffer from grief. As a young child, understanding loss was challenging and confusing; I was deeply saddened by my first experience of losing a family member. Watching how my mother and grandmother supported each other and how they found ways to honor my aunt taught me about perseverance and being appreciative of the joys and sorrows in life. My grandmother passed away when I was 17 years old, and while she may not have realized that I was always learning from her, the generational wealth she provided me was her strength, wisdom, and unforgettable smile. She is my guiding light and inspiration, and has given me the courage to teach and guide my successors.

DISAPPOINTMENTS AND DISCOVERIES

Mentorship is a form of guidance in which one learns valuable lessons and insight from an experienced, skilled person. A mentor could be a personal friend, family member, colleague, supervisor, or employer. My mentors have provided extraordinary help that has shaped the professional I have become. While I primarily have had positive mentors, I once endured a negative experience with mentorship at work. Although the story is unpleasant, the experience provided valuable insight and growth opportunities.

This horrible experience occurred around 15 years ago after securing an adjunct/counseling position at a nearby college. I was looking forward to this job, as I enjoyed the academic environment and wanted to build my skill set, having been in the mental health field for nearly five years. Unfortunately, my direct supervisor undermined me since our first meeting. She made it difficult for me to learn and build my skills, sabotaged my work, and devalued my efforts. After enduring several months of this, my supervisor manipulated me into signing my resignation letter. I felt bullied, and being a young social worker, I remained silent, not wanting to damage my future career. I recall that prior to leaving that position, the supervisor told me that I would not be successful in my future or any professional goals. As I was cleaning out my desk in our shared office, I noticed she had prepared a folder with my ideas in a presentation for the clinic that I had shown her earlier that week. At that moment, I knew I had to speak up. "I noticed you are using my ideas for next semester.

You're welcome," I said and walked out. Although I had plenty of other words to share, I knew my professional boundaries. The experience I endured was intense and painful; I have replayed that situation in my mind countless times, wondering what I could have done differently. I also asked myself if there was a way that I could learn and grow from the experience.

Ultimately, I learned that this negative experience had offered valuable insight and lessons, such as the importance of establishing personal and professional boundaries. Furthermore, it is important to communicate in a way that avoids misunderstandings. Lastly, learning how to execute self-reliance, which is the ability to seek knowledge independently when a supervisor is not supportive. These vital lessons contributed to my personal and professional development.

Upon leaving this toxic position, I questioned myself: Was I worthy, knowledgeable, and competent? Then, the resiliency bestowed upon me by my ancestors kicked in, and I responded by saying, "Claro que sí! I am worthy and knowledgeable!" I quickly learned that paths become disrupted to lead us to a better place. I manifest and can confirm that setbacks are opportunities to think creatively and find innovative solutions to obstacles. In my case, the challenges I faced with my former supervisor pushed me out of my comfort zone, encouraged me to develop new skills, and enabled me to create my own exam prep business. My vision is to create hope and teach you to trust your process no matter what twists and turns might occur. Learning is not linear; your path will lead you to where you are meant to be.

MY COMMUNITY: MY SOCIAL WORKERS

When I think about my community and those that I serve, I think: "my social workers." I can proudly say that while social workers are busy helping their clients, I am busy helping my clients who are, in fact, social workers! It all comes down to social work exam preparation.

I created the Social Work Exam Prep Bootcamp 20 years ago for several reasons. Primarily, I began teaching colleagues how to pass their license exams because it was essential for their careers and livelihoods. Additionally, I was aware of the statistics; I learned from my research that historically, Black and Latino exam takers test within a low range of passing scores. This applies to all standardized exams, including the GRE, SAT, and all professional licensing exams—not just social work. Therefore, I wanted to create a program that was accessible to all types of learners, especially because standardized exams are heavily weighted on reading comprehension. I wanted to make a difference and create an impact in my field, and thus social work exam prep became my niche and purpose.

My first group class consisted of two social work exam takers. Since then, I have helped over 100,000 social workers change their lives for the better. The past 20 years of creating and teaching exam prep have been incredibly self-fulfilling. My experience includes not only teaching about the exam, but also connecting with social workers and empathizing with their particular situations. I have listened to countless social workers share stories about their "why" for social work, their trials and tribulations, the intergenerational obstacles they have faced. Their stories motivate me to continue my work, and I am honored to have the ability to impact their professional lives. I consider my work providing exam prep to be life-changing; I have become a social change agent impacting the lives of social workers. With my tools, I have been guiding and empowering social workers to succeed in their work, projects, and academic goals, helping them meet their overall professional goals.

Separate from my exam prep program, part of my professional mission is to provide valuable knowledge by mentoring other social workers. My mentees include social workers of all different ages and backgrounds. I know that my heritage, especially my grandmother and parents, has paved the way for my interest in mentorship. My past negative experiences have provided insight into navigating unexpected challenges more effectively, and I now have the ability to pass down these lessons to promote generational wealth. Keep in mind that wealth is not limited to money—wealth is knowledge, and knowledge is power and consistency. The generational wealth I received from my abuelita is wisdom and resiliency. With knowledge, you will have the ability to grow and build your future.

Some empowering words I encourage mentees to follow are: embrace your learning journey; be open to learning from unexpected sources and experiences. Build strong relationships: use networking and professional organizations to build long-lasting relationships with colleagues and community partners. Building your community is an asset for necessary support in our field. Also, trust in your abilities and potential; believing in yourself is an essential step in your journey. Finally, celebrate the small wins!

RETURNING AND REFLECTION

I am a returning co-author from Volume One of *Latinx in Social Work,* which launched during the COVID-19 pandemic. Daily life and navigating a career were very different and challenging during the pandemic; however, my co-authors and I strived to build our unique and resilient community. In fact, we still chat almost daily and always support each other in various ways. We have not only built a community, but we consider ourselves social work siblings, *familia.*

I am honored to continue sharing my history, thoughts, and wisdom within this volume. The stories inspire and motivate readers, specifically young Latinx social workers. These narratives are powerful and healing, showing how overcoming adversity, achieving success, and leading change could motivate readers to pursue their dreams. Providing tangible role models for aspiring social workers illustrates pathways to success and fulfillment in the profession—a goal that guides my mentorship as well.

I hope you have been prompted to reflect on your own life and self-discovery while reading part of my journey. I have learned lessons from each experience and share these takeaways so that they provide insight toward your own endeavors. Each decision and step you take, whether small, medium, or large, brings you closer to your dreams. Embrace the journey; it is yours and unique. Learn from every experience, whether positive or negative. Believe in yourself and your potential—you have the ability to become a positive social change agent in your community.

Ancestral Wisdom:

Mi abuelita me decía, "No dejes que las energías negativas interrumpan tu camino."

Journal Prompts:

1. What setbacks have you had in your life and how can you create opportunities from them?
2. How has your self-image impacted your self-worth?
3. Envision your community, and name how it provides you with what you need to move forward.

BIOGRAPHY

Dr. Edith Chaparro is a licensed clinical social worker with a doctorate in psychology and experience in leadership, academic, clinical, mentorship, and education. Dr. Chaparro created the Social Work Exam Prep Bootcamp in 2004 and owns a private practice that provides psychotherapy, immigration psychological evaluations, and court-mandated evaluations, primarily for Spanish-speaking clients. Dr. Chaparro is an adjunct professor at New York University and Columbia University. She provides clinical supervision and professional development workshops for organizations. Dr. Chaparro is the Vice President of the National Association of Social Workers NASW-NYC Board of Directors.

Email: Dr.EdithChaparro@gmail.com
Email: SocialworkBootcamp@gmail.com
Instagram: @Socialworkexambootcamp
Instagram: @Dr.EdithChaparro
Contact #: 917-683-8601

RESIA COOPER, MSW

"Different makes you just who you are, and leaning into our uniqueness and individuality will align us to a path that is greater than us."

ROOTS AND RESILIENCE

Growing up in the heart of inner-city Brooklyn, I always knew I was different. As a Haitian-American pastor's kid, life often felt like a balance between two worlds. On one side was the vibrant, tight-knit Haitian community, and on the other, the dynamic diversity of Brooklyn and American culture. My roots were deeply entrenched in family, faith, and education—three pillars that shaped everything I knew. But the reality was more complex. I was often too Haitian to fit in with my American peers, yet not Haitian enough to fully grasp the deeper cultural nuances that came with my heritage.

This feeling of being caught between two worlds seeped into my daily life, relationships, and even my identity. At family gatherings, I would listen intently as my elders told stories of our homeland, Haiti, and of the revolution that made us the first Black republic. They would speak with pride about our strength and resilience, the sacrifices our ancestors made to secure freedom and sovereignty. But I often felt a disconnect. Though I shared their blood, their language, and their values, I was living in a vastly different world from the one they described.

By the time I was two, I was fluent in three languages, including Haitian Creole, and I quickly became the family translator. I vividly remember the first time I translated for a fellow Haitian family at my daycare. The director was explaining a form they needed to sign, and without hesitation, I stepped in to bridge the communication gap. I was just a child, but in that moment, I felt a sense of pride and responsibility. From that day forward, I promised myself that no matter where life took me, I would honor my heritage. Though I was planted on American soil, my roots would dig deep into the legacy of my ancestors, and I would never forget where I came from.

I looked forward to every summer break in Haiti. Those trips were more than just vacations; they were opportunities to immerse myself in the culture, language, and traditions of my people. Those summers shaped the "who" in my narrative today. In the rich and vibrant atmosphere of Haiti, I started to understand the weight of the legacy I carried.

You see, Haitians—as I was often reminded—come from a legacy of resilience. As descendants of the first Black republic, we carry within us the spirit of revolution, a determination to fight for freedom and thrive despite the odds. My family was no exception, and like many immigrant families, there were expectations placed on me. Success wasn't just encouraged; it was required. For my family, success meant becoming a doctor, lawyer, or engineer—careers that commanded respect and financial stability. For most of my life, I believed that becoming a neurosurgeon was my destiny. The brain fascinated me—its complexities, its power, its role in shaping who we are. It seemed like the perfect career: prestigious, intellectually stimulating, and most importantly, a path that would make my family proud.

For years, I carried this dream with me. I told myself, "This is the path I'm meant to take," not realizing that I was chasing familial expectations rather than my own desires. Every step I took was meticulously planned. I studied hard, excelled in school, and never wavered in my belief that I was destined for medical greatness. But beneath the surface, doubt slowly crept in.

Everything changed when I was 16. My cousin, Raffaella Montfleury, passed away at just 18 years old. Raffaella was more than just my cousin; she was my confidante and role model, the person who taught me to embrace joy and authenticity. She had an infectious zest for life, danced to her own beat, lived fully in every moment, and never apologized for who she was. Her passing was a profound turning point for me, forcing me to question everything. What was the point of chasing a dream that wasn't truly mine? What was the purpose of living if I wasn't being true to myself?

Raffaella's death was a wake-up call. I began to question the life I was building and whether it was truly for myself or to meet someone else's expectations. But even though the seed of doubt had been planted, I still wasn't ready to let go of the dream just yet. I entered college holding on tightly to the idea of becoming a doctor. I convinced myself that once I started my pre-med courses, everything would fall into place. But the more I studied, the more disillusioned I became.

I loved learning, but quickly realized that science and medicine were not my passion. The reality of blood, dissections, and long lab hours made me anxious and uneasy. I started to see cracks in the dream I had carried for so long. I wasn't chasing what I wanted; I was chasing what I thought would make my family proud. The pressure to succeed, to be perfect, was weighing me down. And for the first time in my life, I didn't know if I could keep going.

THE TURNING POINT

In 2011, my world shifted dramatically once again. My father was diagnosed with dementia, and overnight, I went from being his baby girl to his caretaker. I wasn't prepared for the emotional toll it would take on me to watch the man who raised me slip away in small, heartbreaking ways. I witnessed his memory fade, his personality change, and his once-vibrant spirit diminish. The man who had guided me through life was becoming a distant shadow of who he once was. Our deep conversations about success and the future were replaced with quiet moments at doctor's visits, and I found myself grappling with the reality of life's fragility.

As I navigated my father's care, I was introduced to a social worker who transformed my perspective. She wasn't just helping us with logistics—she was guiding us emotionally, offering support that went beyond her job description. Watching her work, I realized that I had been overlooking a profession that aligned perfectly with my natural strengths. My ability to listen, to empathize, to advocate—these were all skills I had honed throughout my life, but I had never considered social work as a career option.

As I reflected on my experience, I began to see how deeply ingrained generational patterns and expectations had shaped my life. Growing up in a Haitian household, emotional vulnerability wasn't something we discussed. Success was measured by external accomplishments, and I had internalized the pressure to be a high achiever. For years, I worked hard to meet the expectations handed down to me, believing that I needed to be perfect in order to succeed.

But as I stepped into my role as a caretaker, I began to realize that my strength didn't lie in perfection. It lay in my ability to adapt, to care for others, and to stand strong even when everything around me felt uncertain. I was no longer striving to be the best for the sake of appearances; I was embracing who I truly was. I was learning that vulnerability, empathy, and authenticity were just as important as success.

It was during this tumultuous time that I decided to pursue social work. The pressures of being a high achiever started to dissolve as I found meaning in envisioning a life dedicated to helping others. I was no longer trying to fit into a mold of perfection; instead, I was embracing the messy, emotional, and deeply human aspects of life.

Once I made the decision to pursue social work, doors began to open. I found mentors who guided me, educational opportunities that aligned with my passions, and a community of like-minded individuals who shared my vision for advocacy and change. Social work allowed me to tap into the best version of myself. It taught me clarity, effective listening, and perhaps most importantly, that empathy wasn't a weakness but a powerful tool for change.

Though I entered the profession as an adult learner, the last three years have been nothing short of transformative. I often hear from others, "You've achieved so much in such a short time," and I attribute that to entering the field with confidence. I knew who I was, and I knew that my skills in advocacy and leadership were invaluable. As a social worker, my goal is to help others find their voice and empower them to stand strong in their truth, just as I've learned to do. I also see the role that organizations play in creating equitable systems, and I strive to hold them accountable for their social responsibility.

REFLECTION: OUR DIFFERENCE IS OUR STRENGTH

Today, I work as a macro social worker, but I will never forget the colleagues who serve families and individuals navigating their own difficult circumstances, just like I once did with my father. I'm constantly reminded that we are all on a journey of growth, and that our uniqueness is our strength. As I continue this work, I'm driven by the desire to help others see that they too can embrace their differences, lean into their strengths, and create a path that feels authentically theirs.

Healing, I've learned, is a continuous process. It's not just about helping others—it's about helping ourselves, too. Practices like mentorship, meditation, journaling, and building a supportive community have been essential tools in my own healing journey. Journaling is an especially powerful tool to envision your future while reflecting on how far you have come. It allows for life to be put on paper, and for thoughts to empower actions. I've learned to pour back into myself, to take time for reflection and rest, and to embrace healing methods that nourish both mind and body.

In the end, my journey is about growth—leaning into the unknown and trusting that each change, no matter how difficult, leads to something greater. As I look ahead, I'm excited for the future of my career in social work. I know that the work I'm doing is impactful, not just for the individuals and families I serve, but for myself as well. Every day is an opportunity to grow, to learn, and to embrace new experiences.

I am grateful for my Padrino, Dr. Juan Rios. Since I met him four years ago, I have been able to see myself through the eyes of someone who sees all my potential. He also supports in sharing how important it is to honor our roots while embracing our power.

Ancestral Wisdom:

L'Union fait la force. (Unity makes strength.)

Journal Prompts:

1. What is a quality that you have been taught is a weakness, but is actually a strength in social work?
2. How do you measure success?

BIOGRAPHY

Resia Cooper, MSW is a first-generation Haitian American, military spouse, mother, and macro social worker with a passion for bridging the gap between social work students and professionals. Resia is currently an Engagement Coordinator at the National Association of Social Workers New Jersey and Delaware chapter. She is also the founder of Social Work Student Success Solutions, a consultant firm that supports future and current social work students from application to graduation.

A New York native and Fordham Graduate School of Social Services alum, Resia prides herself on promoting human rights, justice, and access for all. As a teacher by nature, she is also a Google I Am Remarkable facilitator and offers free empowerment webinars.

FROM TRIALS TO TRIUMPH: A LEGACY OF STRENGTH AND BLOSSOMING

DR. JESSICA HARDIAL, MA, LCSW, CCTP, PHD(C)

"Helping Spanish-speaking clients, providing gender-affirming surgery support letters, accepting insurance, and providing low-cost services make a difference for folks who feel lost and helpless."

THE JOURNEY TO DOCTORA: A LETTER TO MY YOUNGER SELF

To my younger self: You did it. Not only did you set the path by being the first in your family to graduate high school, obtain an associate's degree, a bachelor's degree, and a master's degree, but you *phi-nished* that PhD. It was a long, exhausting road, but you did it. Doctora. The title I have earned. Doctora Jessica Hardial. How my younger self wanted that title but never thought she would come close.

Working full time and completing my dissertation was challenging. My wife, Damaris, has always supported my goals and dreams—she was the one who opened my acceptance letter to Fordham University's social work program in 2013. While getting my master's degree, I worked full time at Saint Dominic's Home in the Bronx as a case planner for children in foster care. I studied and worked during the weekdays and spent many Saturdays from sunup to sundown in the library studying and writing papers. I remember working all morning, taking my lunch break to go to class (eating a sandwich on the 6 train), attending class in the afternoon, heading back to work for another five hours, and not getting home until after 9 p.m. As crazy as it seems, that schedule was just routine for me. When I wanted to give up, Damaris stood by me.

After graduation, I was a school social worker at a middle school in East New York, hoping to make a difference with the dropout rate among foster care students. Each day, I felt the difference I was making in the lives of young children and worked with the leadership team to help students achieve their full potential. Having seen firsthand the gap that exists for foster care students in education, I started to think about applying to a PhD program to study foster care and education more closely. Damaris and I had just moved to our first apartment, and returning to school was a big decision for us, emotionally and financially. Nonetheless, she supported me and continued to believe in me.

THE ROLLERCOASTER

When I first applied to PhD programs, I didn't get accepted. My father-in-law and I spoke at length about my ability and re-applying. I felt defeated and didn't want to get rejected again. But he didn't give up on me. See, from the moment I met my father-in-law in 2012, he had always made me feel a part of his family and saw something in me. I applied again and got accepted into Adelphi's social work PhD program.

Two years into the program another challenge hit—this time, the comprehensive exams. Test-taking was never my strong suit, but I studied and studied, and I passed three of the four exams. I was given one more chance to take the last exam, so I got private tutoring and continued to study. But I failed again. I was dismissed from the program. I was angry and devastated, and thought maybe a PhD wasn't meant for me.

Despite the academic devastation I was facing, there were so many other exciting things happening in my life. Damaris and I got married. We bought our first house. And I got my first job as an adjunct professor at SUNY Old Westbury, all as I advanced in my full-time role as a school social worker. My father-in-law reminded me every time I saw him to apply to another PhD program. I was afraid of being rejected, of failing again. But within a year of being dismissed from Adelphi's program, I found another PhD program that didn't require the comprehensive exams, just a comprehensive essay. This program accepted all my transfer credits and allowed me to receive a master's degree en route.

During this time, I passed my clinical exam and became a clinical social worker. Simultaneously, I opened a solo private practice, while still working full-time as a school social worker, being a part-time adjunct professor, and finishing my PhD coursework. I received my second master's degree in April 2021 in human development. I completed my coursework and after two tries, passed my comprehensive essay. I finally moved on to the dissertation phase, and for the first time, I felt comfortable taking the risk of quitting my school social worker job and transitioning my solo private practice to a full-time group practice.

BLOSSOMING LOTUS THERAPY

In July of 2021, Blossoming Lotus Therapy was born. I chose the lotus because it reflects my childhood experiences— despite the muddy surroundings (challenges and obstacles), the lotus produces the most beautiful flower (us). It was the perfect name for my business. As a proud queer Latina, I understand needing to find the right fit as a client and as an employee. I founded Blossoming Lotus Therapy as a safe space for BIPOC and queer folks to feel seen by finding peace and healing while blossoming into their best selves. Our team of queer therapists of color integrate their identities and lived experience into affirming treatment. Helping Spanish-speaking clients, providing gender-affirming surgery support letters, accepting insurance, and providing low-cost services make a difference for folks who feel lost and helpless.

As a small business owner, I leaned into courage and attentiveness. Being a leader and a boss can be challenging when trying to balance finances, company needs, employee satisfaction, and client wellness. I have learned that not all people share the same work ethic and values I carry as a social worker, an individual, and a social agent of change. Guiding and mentoring my staff in this important work is purposeful. Identifying each individual's strengths and having open communication leads to successful company operations. I hope to continue to blossom in this work and share my wisdom with the next generation of social workers.

Reflecting on the importance of creating a business that allows folks to feel safe, I came to understand my passion for foster care and supporting children who are marginalized by society, with no control of what happens to them. I felt deeply that I could have been a foster care child if someone had noticed the abuse in my home. My escape from home was school and excelling in my educational career. The connection between foster care and education is impactful, and I wanted to share what I learned, share my experience, and demand change. I gained so much experience working in the foster care and educational sectors, but something was missing. So during the recruitment process of my dissertation journey, Damaris and I became foster parents. We wanted to provide a loving and supportive home for children in the foster care system, even if it was temporary.

In August of 2022, Estefany joined our family. It wasn't planned, and it happened very quickly, but it was God's plan. Estefany joined our family at the tender age of 15, but she had already encountered so much life experience before she came into our home. The transition of becoming parents for the first time to a teenager was huge. Parenting an adolescent is a skill in and of itself, and parenting an adolescent with no prior parenting experience is another level of parenting. Damaris and I leaned on each other and meshed our individual experiences to provide a loving and supportive home for Estefany.

This is the family we have created and continue to build together. Estefany's story is complex, and she should share her story and perspective someday if she chooses, as she is its rightful author. For now, I can speak to how proud we are of her and her accomplishments. As she prepares herself for college, we hope she continues to thrive, knowing she has us, two mothers who love her unconditionally and will always support her.

I had spent so many years studying foster care from the outside, but as foster parents, we are learning the challenges of the system from a different lens. In turn, my passion for studying the experiences of foster care alumni grew, and I wanted to share those experiences with the world. My dissertation was a phenomenological study that explored the lived experiences of foster care alumni's career intentions after college. I was particularly interested in learning if foster care alumni chose helping professions. You would have to read the study yourself to find out if there were any correlations. My study reinforced the need for change in these broken systems and connected my experiences as a social worker, the experiences of foster care alumni, and the experiences of foster parents. I hope to use my title, Doctor, to add to the knowledge base and elicit change from my research. The pride I feel to do this work and continue to add to my father-in-law's legacy as a Hardial is immeasurable.

To my team at Blossoming Lotus Therapy, my students, and Natalie my mentee: as a Madrina, I am honored to be an inspiration. By sharing stories of failing forward, we honor the truth about growth. Just like the lotus, through the muddiest waters, we find ways to blossom. Never dim your light and never give up. I believe in all of you.

Ancestral Wisdom:

Mija, nunca te olvides del poder que tienes como mujer.

Journal Prompts:
1. What setbacks have helped you fail forward, and how?
2. What are some qualities and skills you admire in leadership?
3. How do you manage your time while staying present in each role that you carry?

BIOGRAPHY

Dr. Jessica Hardial is a bilingual mental health practitioner, clinical supervisor, proud author of Latinx/e in Social Work, workshop facilitator, adjunct professor, and Board Member of Siembra Today. Dr. Hardial is the founder and CEO of Blossoming Lotus Therapy, where she oversees a team of mental health professionals who provide ongoing support to individuals and families. Blossoming Lotus Therapy was founded to help BIPOC & Queer folx find a space to be seen and heard. Dr. Hardial's practice is geared toward LGBTQIA+ community members and their families, the foster care and adoption population, as well as non-monogamous folx and Black, Indigenous People of Color. Dr. Hardial's expertise encompasses trauma, anxiety, and family conflict, utilizing a somatic and psychodynamic oriented approach. She contributes to the social work profession by offering supervision to graduate and postgraduate students to enhance their clinical skills of how to be affirming and competent in working with marginalized communities.

She holds her associates degree from CUNY Borough of Manhattan Community College, her bachelor's degree from CUNY Queens College, her master's degree in Social Work from Fordham University, her second master's degree in Human Development from Fielding Graduate University and her Doctorate of Philosophy from Fielding Graduate University.

As a queer woman of color, Dr. Hardial draws from her clinical experiences and leadership skills to cultivate a safe space and foster connections in her work as a speaker, facilitator, and entrepreneur. She has been featured on Canvas Rebel, Latina CUNY TV, and more.

Blossominglotustherapy.com|

Facebook & Instagram: @Blossominglotustherapy

Linked In: https://www.linkedin.com/in/jessica-hardial-ma-lcsw-ph-d-c-0aa53a46/

MARIANA LOPEZ, LCSW-R

"Each individual, regardless of their condition, has the potential to improve themselves."

FOSTERING RESILIENCE AT THE CROSSROADS OF CHANGE

Mija, tú eres inteligente… tú puedes. "You're smart, you can do it," were the first of my father's words that resonated in my head. I remember him bragging to his friends how I read above age level as I pored over a book. I enjoyed reading, even though reading was not often encouraged nor did I grow up surrounded by books or accessible libraries.

I was born in a small village in the Amazon in Ecuador, surrounded by nature, high trees, and exotic rivers of different water colors. In this small town mostly everyone knows each other; if they don't know you, they know your parents. Afternoons by the river were moments of serenity, where the whispers of the water spoke of dreams and possibilities. I learned to deeply appreciate the environment and I still carry my love of nature with me.

Life lessons arrived early for me. At eleven, my parents separated, and my father left without a farewell. His departure created an emptiness, with his last words, "I love you," echoing in my memory. In my childhood brain, his words were confusing because they didn't match his actions—he said he loved me, but he left me. I'd spend hours waiting by the window, hoping for the familiar sound of his truck, only to be disappointed each time. My mother's move to the United States two years later deepened my feelings of abandonment.

At fifteen, faced with an unexpected pregnancy, I felt the world closing in. I attended a strict Catholic school that implied pregnant girls shouldn't return. I was lost in a sea of negativity, criticized and shamed, at a time when I should have felt joy. In my small town, there were no social workers or support services to turn to; only harsh voices telling me my life was over. But I clung to my father's assurance—*tú puedes,* "You can do it"—finding strength and comfort as I spoke to the new life within me. These were my moments of solitude, filled with hopeful whispers that I could carve a new path for myself.

Those were lonely days, when I craved conversation, but there was no one to listen. Cradling my growing belly, I would talk and cry with my unborn son, affirming that he was now my world, arriving precisely when I needed him most. My drive to support him overpowered everything else. It was then that I heard my inner voice echo, "You can do it." Even though I didn't fully grasp what lay ahead, I recognized these words as a chant for courage.

Because I had a child, I was not able to return to Catholic school. My mother suggested that I come to the United States to reunite with her and search for better opportunities. The move to the United States marked a plunge into the unknown. I left my young son in Ecuador, like many immigrant families separated from their loved ones. Upon arrival, I discovered I was pregnant with my daughter, which increased my anxiety about being able to support my children. I began feeling guilty for leaving my son behind, and my only hope was that we would be together again soon. Three years later, the reunion with my son—the boy who changed everything—completed the picture of my life. His presence renewed my sense of purpose.

It was in the United States, a foreign land, where I encountered a compassionate social worker at Bellevue Hospital who unknowingly planted the seed of my future career. Her unwavering support sparked something in me. Curiously, I asked what her job was. "I'm a social worker," she replied. A silent wish formed in my heart: *I hope to be a social worker too.*

At the time, becoming a social worker seemed like a distant

dream. My mother, shaped by her own experiences, held the belief that hard work was more important than formal education and urged me to work diligently to provide for my children. And so, with determination, I embraced the responsibility of supporting my family. I secured employment in a factory, taking the first steps in acclimating to a lifestyle vastly different from the one I had known in my hometown. It was a stark contrast, but I felt the pull to follow in the footsteps of my mother and other family members who had improved their lives through sheer hard work.

Yet, in quiet moments, I heard the echo of my father's encouragement: "Tú puedes." The regret of leaving my studies behind weighed heavily on me, and I clung to the hope of returning to school. Riding the L train to the factory, I saw people my age heading to classes, and I yearned for that same opportunity. It was during these rides that I came to understand the uniqueness of my own journey. I realized that my soul was truly craving the chance to go back to school and fulfill my dreams. This realization fueled my determination and hope, making me aware that my path, though different, was leading me towards a future where I could achieve my aspirations.

A PATH OF GROWTH AND GIVING

I turned my focus to education, recognizing it as the key to reshaping both my future and my children's. As a non-traditional student with full living expenses, including childcare, I chose a vocational path that offered the flexibility I needed. Juggling single motherhood and work, I earned my cosmetology license.

Each haircut was a snip away from a predestined life; in my living room-turned-hair salon, I was sculpting new beginnings, not just hairstyles.

The salon became more than just a place for beauty—it evolved into a sanctuary for sharing and healing. Through the stories of my clients, I was performing a different kind of social work, weaving the early strands of my future career.

While working part-time and studying full-time, I pursued an associate degree at LaGuardia Community College in accounting, a subject I was familiar with from my education in Ecuador. However, in my spare time, I was drawn to psychology. It was a conversation with a business professor, as I neared the completion of my accounting degree, that redirected my path. She asked me reflective questions about my childhood passions, my teenage aspirations, and what truly fulfilled me.

After that pivotal discussion, I switched my major to Mental Health. It delayed my graduation by a year, but confirmed my conviction that I was on the right path. I landed my first job at an after-school program. My desire to learn and support others propelled me to understand every facet of the position, leading to my eventual role as the program director.

In my pursuit of social work, I took on multiple other jobs to broaden my experience. My early experience as an unprepared mother forged a deep connection with parents who had to set aside their dreams for their children. This led me to become a facilitator for the Nurturing Parenting program, where I provided parenting classes. I noticed how parents were receptive to these classes and keen to learn.

After completing my associate's degree, I worked full-time in social services while maintaining a part-time job as a hairstylist. Even when I was accepted at NYU as an undergraduate, I continued to work full-time, arranging my job around my school schedule. My journey at NYU marked the flowering of my passion. There, amidst a cohort of 35, I was the sole Latina, a distinction that underscored the magnitude of my achievement. Doubts initially clouded my excitement—I even questioned the validity of my acceptance. When I shared my concerns with my advisor, she offered congratulations and suggested I frame the acceptance letter as a testament to my success. Despite feeling out of place—as a single mother with an accent, without the luxury of time for extracurriculars—I embraced the opportunity. The full scholarship to the Applied Psychology program was not merely a compliment for my academic endeavors; it signified a turning point, affirming that my past circumstances would not determine my future possibilities. I graduated with honors and proudly presented my research at the senior conference, marking the culmination of my efforts and the beginning of a promising career in social work.

After obtaining my bachelor's degree, I continued at NYU for my Master's in Social Work, aspiring to become a psychotherapist. I dedicated my efforts to providing psychotherapy to children, adolescents, and adults. My time as a school social worker enriched my expertise in child development and special education—knowledge that now underpins my role as a Mental Health Consultant in preschools.

HEALING, HELPING, AND EMPOWERING

In the parenting classes I conducted, it was not just the immigrant families who were learning—I was too. It was a shared space for communal growth, where mothers often grappled with the challenges of parenting and managing multiple responsibilities. Our collective experiences—filled with stories, tears, and resilience—led to profound growth for us all. This journey propelled me to become a Trainer/Consultant, guiding other professionals to impart the nurturing wisdom of the parenting programs.

In 2014, I founded Lifeskills Counseling Services, a mental health clinic that stands as a testament to the countless individuals who seek understanding, comfort, and improvement. What started as a small private practice in Queens, while I kept my full-time job, today serves thousands of clients across Brooklyn, Queens, and Hempstead.

In my role as a mental health consultant, I bring my expertise to the cradle of development—schools. My approach is enriched by empathy from personal experiences of family separation and reunion. When I complete immigration evaluations, I see my own past reflected in the families facing potential separation.

Witnessing new professionals embrace social work with fervor mirrors the passion that has fueled my own journey. Among them, my daughter stands out, having been by my side throughout my own academic pursuits. Now, she not only administers the clinic but also carries on the legacy of caring for individuals with dedication. Her professional journey has been a source of immense pride.

The once-soft whispers of encouragement that sustained me in the past have grown into a robust voice that speaks through my work today. My legacy is woven through the lives I've touched, the shared cultural experiences, and our mutual journey toward healing. My passion is to lift others, share in their victories, and foster their wellbeing.

REFLECTION

Reflecting on my story, it's clear how profoundly my father's belief has directed my life. His words, "Mija, tú eres inteligente… tú puedes," have resonated as a powerful force through my toughest times. This reflection has led me to consider the decisive role that a belief instilled in childhood can play in one's life path.

As I look back on my journey from the greenery of the Amazon to the academic corridors of NYU, my father's voice appears as a beacon, illuminating the path when the road ahead seemed clouded in darkness. What does this tell us about the power of affirmation and the strength we can draw from our roots?

Even as I navigated the challenges of adolescence, family separation, and the complexity of new beginnings, his belief in me became my belief in myself. It's extraordinary how the seeds of encouragement, sown in the fertile soil of a young mind, can blossom into a life rich with purpose and service.

This reflection prompts me to ask deep, personal questions: How have the voices from my past influenced who I am today and who I will become tomorrow? How can I be that nurturing voice that offers strength to others on their path? In a world rich with diverse stories, how can my own experiences foster growth, healing, and empowerment within my community?

My legacy is not just found in the titles I've held or the awards I've received. It lies in the lives touched by my work, the stories intertwined with mine, and the collective healing we've journeyed through. This is what fuels my passion to uplift, to celebrate each triumph, and to nurture the growth of every soul on their path to wellness. My story is a testament to the power of belief, the resilience of the human spirit, and the infinite potential within us all to rise above our circumstances and thrive.

Ancestral Wisdom:

You are your own creator, and you are the medicine you need.

Journal Prompts:
1. Was there a difficult time in your life that you thought you could not move past? What supported you to thrive?
2. How has an inner child wound impacted your adulthood and relationships?
3. What are some challenges that you can reframe to include resilience?
4. How can you use your education to empower yourself and others?

BIOGRAPHY

Originally from Ecuador, Mariana is a social worker, executive director, psychotherapist, mental health consultant in schools, clinical supervisor, and mother of three with over 20 years of service in the field of mental health and social services, with a focus on early childhood development, special education interventions, and clinical interventions to improve relationships and prevent domestic violence.

Mariana is the founder and CEO of Lifeskills Counseling Services, a mental health clinic renowned for providing culturally sensitive care to thousands of families in Queens, Brooklyn, and Hempstead. She is also the Founder and Executive Director of the nonprofit Centro Comunitario Hispano.

She completed her academic studies at LaGuardia Community College, New York University (NYU), and Harvard University.

SOCIAL WORK LEADERSHIP: A LATINA BUILDING A PATH FOR FUTURE GENERATIONS OF SOCIAL WORKERS

ROSITA L. MARINEZ, MS-NPL, ADV-CSW, SIFI

A leader encourages and empowers people to take a fearless approach to life by enabling them to achieve their potential purposefully.

A UNIQUE JOURNEY AND PURPOSE

We all have a destined purpose. Life's journey is unique to each person, and we all aim to leave a legacy that our family is *orgulloso* of. Throughout my career as a social worker, I found my purpose to be a transformational, visionary, and servant leader addressing macro issues, particularly in housing, mental health, and health care, from a social justice lens. Reflecting on my journey while writing this chapter, I also realized the importance of mentorship in social work.

Since 2023, I have become an executive for a large behavioral healthcare organization in New York City. In 2021, when I wrote my chapter for Volume II of *Latinx/e in Social Work,* I sought to enter an executive role and felt then that my eagerness to join an elite space would take me a lifetime. Yet my journey to fulfill my destined purpose came sooner than expected. It was a whirlwind of experiences and feelings, and I am still trying to unravel all the emotions of being an executive in the public eye. There isn't a manual on how to navigate such public scrutiny in these roles.

My leadership journey has been unconventional, with no specific instructions other than my drive, motivation, and passion for creating social change, breaking barriers, fighting for equity, and being the voice of those who are unheard. As a seasoned social worker and executive, supporting the new generation of social workers is an integral part of my work. I prioritized this area in my practice to always give back by supporting, coaching, and mentoring incoming leaders into the profession.

On this journey, life led me to meet several rising social workers and non-profit professionals. Being a mentor is an incredible honor. For this book, I am happy to be the Madrina to Pilar O. Bonilla, MSW; I am guided by our shared interests in macro issues and promoting equity in social work practice. Both of us are interested in social justice issues, which has drawn us to continue the vital work in this area, which is much needed.

SUCCESS ISN'T AN EASY PATH

There is a saying, "If you have never failed, you have never lived." Part of our journey is experiencing setbacks or failures, but we do not often discuss them due to shame. The fear of failure also sometimes stems from perfectionism. During my setbacks, professionally and personally, my experiences have helped me to overcome and succeed through self-reflection, growth, positivity, and never giving up. Some setbacks have included not getting an executive promotion when I worked harder than anyone else and being overlooked because of what I represent. Another setback has been taking a break for myself or my family to manage life-changing events. But now, looking back, these weren't setbacks but rather preparation for what the future held. We all strive to be the best in our field, but being the best doesn't mean being perfect.

In our culture, achievements are highly celebrated and praised, while setbacks are considered your fault for something you did wrong or not trying your best. As a society, we focus only on success and strive to do anything to get to the top. I do not believe in taking a relentless approach and sacrificing human dignity to meet your own selfish needs. My setbacks have taught me great life lessons and made me into the person I am today. From my setbacks, I was able to pick myself up and have an intensive drive to prevail more than ever.

EXPLORING AREAS OF CONCENTRATION

In the early years of my career, when trying to find my niche between macro and micro, I explored different areas of specialization, such as mental health, health care, and gerontology. I decided to start in the healthcare system from a mezzo-level perspective. I accepted a job at a well-known hospital in New York City to provide patients with HIV/AIDS supportive services, working with the hospital to expand the program's model across New York City. I was also the only Latina social worker for the outpatient clinic, and my priority was expanding linguistic and cultural services. Working in the hospital setting helped me understand the multi-complexities of the healthcare system and gain the experience necessary to prepare for future endeavors.

Since my initial start in the healthcare system, my journey has led me to explore the areas of workforce development, mental health, substance use, and now the housing sector at an executive level. As an executive social worker, I am invested in working on macro issues that impact community accessibility to the most basic needs. You might ask yourself why I emphasize the "social work executive" aspect. This is because I want to convey the message in my chapter to social workers who aspire to do macro work that they *can* be executives and leaders for our communities. Unfortunately, less than 1 percent of social workers, especially Latinas, enter an executive space. We can be told we're dreaming too big or be afraid to enter spaces that make us feel uncomfortable. We need more of us to represent at an executive level and organizational governance, to have a seat at the table, and to be the voice for our community, which we serve every day.

THE NEED FOR LATINO SOCIAL WORKERS

Latinos immigrate to the United States for several reasons, such as fleeing from war, violence, dictatorship, national disasters, or economic stability. Despite us now being the largest group of color in the United States, representing 19 percent of the population, we face inaccessibility to healthcare, education, and housing. There is a high need for more Latino social workers to address the gap in services and systematic barriers.

During COVID-19, frontline social workers were lifelines keeping underserved and marginalized communities afloat with the necessary resources. There has always been a lack of recognition for social workers, but this has become more evident than ever. After the pandemic, many social workers abruptly transitioned to virtual services or private mental health practice. The Bureau of Labor Statistics predicts a substantial deficit of 74,000 social workers each year for the next decade. Yet the high demand for social services continues to rise, and there is a great need for social workers, especially Latinos.

The aftermath of the pandemic has had immense detrimental effects on social workers entering the profession, such as higher debt loans, higher caseloads, no salary growth, and questioned moral inquiry. There has been an increase in social workers entering clinical private practice and less into mezzo and macro practices, impacting community service gaps. Our profession must encourage more macro social workers and value the importance of their dedication and passion. Seasoned social workers like me who have been in the profession for a substantial time—as I like to call the "old guard of social workers"—need to provide guidance, support, and empowerment to the "new guard of social workers" to help them navigate the complexities of social work practice with confidence and competence.

THE IMPORTANCE OF BUILDING A STRONG SOCIAL WORK COMMUNITY

New social workers entering the profession are particularly vulnerable to exiting the field within their first five years of practice. Social workers develop their professional identity during this period and are more susceptible to imposter syndrome and loss of confidence. This is why building a community and fostering mentorship is essential for the sustainability of our profession. New social workers require peer support, guidance, advice, and training. Plus, they benefit from networking, which decreases isolation and helps them find a community to support their growth.

Reflecting on my early career as a social worker, I experienced a lack of guidance and support, with no one to turn to for advice. I felt isolated, and many experienced colleagues were gatekeeping information and resources. This lack of support and knowledge-sharing was demoralizing and confusing. Years later, these things still exist. As I advanced in my career, I told myself I did not want new social workers to have similar experiences to mine. I acquired my Seminar in Field Instruction (SIFI) certification to give back, educate, train, and provide coaching to future social workers. During my career, I have supervised first-

and second-year MSW graduate students in different programs in New York City.

There is a saying in our culture: "El poder de la comunidad es más fuerte que el obstáculo." I strongly believe in building a community to support and uplift each other. We can no longer work in silos where we encounter burnout, moral injury, low wages, workplace risks, attrition, and lack of recognition. There is strength in numbers; we must unite as a community to continue advocating for equitable conditions.

Over the years, I have found different professional support systems and communities in the nonprofit sector. However, I did not have a community where I could relate to individuals from similar backgrounds and experiences until I found *Latinx/e in Social Work*. Many Hispanic/Latinx/e social workers have felt isolated, and there's a high need for integration in nuestra comunidad. By connecting with more of our hermanos y hermanas, we can break the barriers of isolation, gatekeeping, and lack of support. We will create and support our future social workers to continue the service delivery for our community.

MENTORSHIP AND THE FUTURE GENERATION OF LEADERS

When I embarked on my social work journey, I did not have the mentorship or advice of a social worker, nonprofit executive, or academic scholar. During my graduate training, I did not receive information or preparation for entering the complexity of the workforce. And in my early career, I did not have other Hispanic/

Latinx/e social workers to guide, support, coach, or mentor me. I was a young professional who wanted to change the world and be a social change agent for the greater good. Yet I found myself having to navigate the complexities of the profession by myself, trying to succeed in a world that I wasn't familiar with. If you are feeling this way, remember: You are not alone, and we are doing this together.

Mentorship is vital to our work, especially for Hispanic/Latinx/e social workers, because we can change the narrative that social workers cannot be executives or that we don't need them. After all, they do need us. Mentors encourage and empower, facilitate critical personal and professional development, transfer knowledge, and develop social capital. As I grew and matured professionally and personally, I became focused on investing in up-and-coming social workers to help them navigate similar experiences. Now a seasoned social worker and executive leader, I am responsible for investing in our future social work leaders to sustain and save our profession.

REFLECTION

As a community, we must continue to empower and invest in our MSW students and future leaders. We are all responsible for saving the profession and ensuring that our future social workers can continue the critical work our communities need. We must also invest in our future leaders by providing leadership development training, fellowships, and coaching. All these areas need to be accessible to provide our future social workers with the tools necessary to succeed. Like I say: We are in this together to create change.

Ancestral Wisdom:

Talk less, listen with heart, be fearless, and lead with passion.

Journal Prompts:

1. What obstacles have you faced that have turned into opportunities?
2. What have you learned from elders and mentors that have supported your growth?
3. Close your eyes and imagine what your ideal social work career would look like. Now write it down on paper or create a vision board.

BIOGRAPHY

Rosita Marinez is the Senior Vice President of Supported Housing at the Institute for Community Living. She oversees the nation's most extensive NY OMH housing portfolio for individuals with serious mental illness and co-occurring disorders. Her focus areas of practice are mental health, substance use, HIV/AIDS, and housing. She is also a board member of the nonprofit Siembra Today.

Rosita has a Master of Science in Nonprofit Leadership from Fordham University and a Master of Social Work from The Silberman School of Social Work. She is a George and Belle Strell Executive Leadership fellow and a John Harford Scholar.

rosita.marinez@iclinc.net
LinkedIn: linkedin.com/in/rosita-marinez-a1443966
Instagram: @Rosita.Marinez

Afterword

Latinx/e in Social Work, Vol. III opens a discussion regarding mentoring provided not only to early career professionals, but also to existing social workers. Mentorship is not supervision, but rather an opportunity to offer support. This book highlights the importance of opportunities to connect with seasoned professionals at both the clinical and macro levels who are committed to fostering personal and professional growth. Mentees seek someone who can bring them to the next level of social work and discuss job-related issues, resumes, licensing, and testing concerns without leaving out the personal challenges of the social work career. This is not to mention the world of sponsorship, where mentors sponsor career advancement by helping others develop a marketing strategy, gain exposure, engage with a new audience, and connect with other sponsors. At all levels and careers, mentoring is purposeful, conscious, and a relationship often driven by a deep sense of commitment.

In my experience, I have seen that the essence of individuals finding themselves in the world of social work is often quietly preempted by the Greek philosopher Plato's ideology that "necessity is the mother of invention." This proverb suggests that when we face a pressing need or problem, we are most likely to come up with creative inventions and solutions. A strong need drives innovation and ingenuity to overcome the related challenges. When mentoring, sponsoring, and supporting one another in the Latinx/e community, we must do so with the same compassion and love we would offer any other client or group. Too often we negatively serve one another as if that would serve us better overall. Community is important, mentoring each other is crucial, and sponsoring one another is ultimately the best support we can practice. Paying it forward is the number-one action we can all offer when we want to advance our cause and honor our roots. Ultimately, advocating for our community through social work entails advocating for strategies and influencing policies that benefit our communities.

The growth of every social worker starts from within at a very early age, often with a need to become leaders and connect deeply with others. For first-generation social workers, the ideology noted above serves to navigate the fire that burns early on in their lives in order to become the leaders they are. When you receive the grace of mentorship, it is important to understand it does not stop with you—pass it to the next young social worker who needs support and confidence, who can pass it on to the next person, and so forth.

Many years ago, after I was beyond my beginner social work period, I realized that just like a not-for-profit, if I wanted to thrive beyond mentorship, I needed to have a personal "board of directors" who would help me along the way with creative mentoring and career-building strategies. As times change, we need to adapt accordingly, and as an experienced social worker who was a well-regarded and respected mentor to many of my peers, I had to lead complex efforts to implement comprehensive strategic plans and restructure core aspects of my department.

It required extensive networking and communication, delicate negotiations, respectful confrontations, and very high levels of trust with everyone involved. Like many, I had to learn to understand my work as a process of mentoring within a network of individuals committed to professional development not only for themselves but also for me.

Connecting with others through the lens of the mentor-mentee relationship, where roles are often complex and reciprocal, creates numerous opportunities for learning and educating. That is why having a personal board of directors as the structural framework helped me navigate this critical moment. This self-developed virtual personal board of directors has grown into a constantly evolving matrix of brilliant, wonderful individuals to whom I can reach out at any time to help me evolve.

The role of the mentor is to develop strong dialogue with the mentee and create ways to address complex social issues that are often traumatic to our community, if not ourselves. It is not easy to be a social worker and keep up the resilience, compassion, and commitment needed to support both our own well-being as well as that of our clients. I come from a long line of women who, although they weren't social workers, were active in their communities. They reminded me that I could not go and clean someone else's home if mine was not already clean. That is why I recognize the need to have my own group of mentors, my personal board of directors that keep me grounded even in the worst of moments.

Being a mentor or sponsor is a big responsibility for those who take it seriously and want to make a difference. As an older professional, I connect with and support other social workers to help them meet their passion and excel in the field. Remember to not let these empathic interventions take hold of you to the extent that mentoring consumes you to your detriment. As a conqueror with a path of mentoring and helping others, it is crucial to share that empowerment beyond your mentee and yourself.

A good mentor gets excited about who they see you becoming without losing sight of who you are. A great mentor helps you move forward and dive deeper to your best self.

Lynda Perdomo-Ayala, MSW, LMSW, CLC

Chair of Suffolk County Human Rights

Chair of Suffolk County Interfaith Anti-Bias Task Force

Treasurer, National Association of the Puerto Rican and Hispanic Social Workers, Inc.

Retired, Administrative Department Head, Department of Pharmacological Sciences, Renaissance School of Medicine at Stony Brook University

About the Author
Erica Priscilla Sandoval, LCSW, SIFI

ABOUT THE AUTHOR

Erica Priscilla Sandoval, LCSW, SIFI is an award-winning social worker, speaker, executive coach, entrepreneur, podcaster, philanthropist, and author. She is the creator of the book series *Latinx/e in Social Work,* which received an honorable mention at the 24th annual International Latino Book and Film Awards.

Erica was four years old when she left Ecuador and arrived in New York City with her mom. She did not know she was going to face some of the hardest experiences in her life in her quest for success and to become the person she is today. All she knew was her desire to make an impact in her community and connect deeply with others—and she did. Today, Erica is a healer by heart and a social worker with the mission to guide and support others in their healing journey.

Little by little, mentors appeared to guide her on this new journey. She realized that she had the power to change the narrative of her life. She realized that she did not have to be a victim as an immigrant and single mother. She realized that she had the power of transforming her reality. Through education, mentorship, and intentional work, she found herself in a beautiful ecosystem that she created, and every day the sun shone brighter. Her goals began to manifest right before her eyes, and she believed more and more in the power of her dreams.

As a proud immigrant from Ecuador, her passion is fueled by supporting her community. Her greatest pride is being a single mother and raising her daughter, Isabella, whom she considers her biggest teacher. Now a conqueror, a guerrera with a trajectory of impact, she is ready to inspire the next generation of social workers.

Erica is most recently the Executive Director of Siembra Today, a women-run, BIPOC-led nonprofit devoted to providing accessible mental health and wellness support through narrative storytelling, books, workshops, healing circles, conferences, and social media campaigns. Siembra Today's goal is to destigmatize and promote mental health and wellness for the Latino/a/x/e and BIPOC community, so that they can plant seeds of hope for themselves and future generations.

She is also the founder and CEO of Sandoval Psychotherapy Consultation—known as Sandoval CoLab—which offers talk therapy, ketamine-assisted psychotherapy (KAP), and holistic offerings. In 2020, Erica became the first immigrant Latina president of the National Association of Social Workers' New York City chapter. She is now the chapter's President Emeritus.

Erica holds a Post Master's in Clinical Adolescent Psychology and a Master's in Social Work from New York University, Silver School of Social Work.

Instagram: @ericapriscillas

LinkedIn: https://www.linkedin.com/in/ericapsandoval/

https://www.siembratoday.org/

https://www.ericapriscilla.com/

https://www.sandovalcolab.com/